Stories I
Need to Tell

Vol. 2

SCREENPLAYS BY DOUGLAS KING

DAY III
Productions
film • publishing • events

ISBN: 978-1-7350083-3-2

www.DayIIIProd.com

DAY
III
Productions
film • publishing • events

INTRODUCTION

I have been writing screenplays professionally for three decades. In that time, I have written scripts I am immensely proud of, and others that, well, let's just say, the fact they never saw the silver screen is probably a good thing for all parties concerned. I have written for major studios, independent studios, independent producers as well as my own spec scripts, some of which you hold in our hands now.

Screenplays by their very essence are just stories presented in a format that makes them accessible for other creative individuals (directors, costume designers, set designers and actors, to name a few) to produce a motion picture or television show. As most writers know, getting a spec screenplay sold and produced into a film is tantamount to winning the lottery. The odds may actually be better to win the lottery.

In light of this, and despite this, I have continued to write my screenplays for many reasons. First, I truly love the process and enjoy breaking story, developing character and plot and working out the story beats. Second, call me delusional, but there is an optimistic part of me that still believes these scripts may be sold and produced one day, which ultimately leads me to my final reason for what some might say is a sadomasochistic endeavor, I must tell these stories.

These stories, characters, settings and themes have burrowed themselves so deeply into my mind and psyche that if I do not release them onto the page, like a geothermal geyser, they would simply burst forth through the mantel of my mind causing who knows what type of irreparable damage.

What you hold in your hands is the product of many years of writing. Each volume in this series includes two spec screenplays of stories I have to tell. It has become a moral imperative that I release these stories to the public. And, if they are not made into the films they are meant to mature into, transitioning from a caterpillar to a beautiful butterfly, then at least they can be enjoyed in their pupa form within the pages of this book.

I hope you enjoy these stories. If you do and if you would like to see them metamorphosize into what they can be—a life action feature film—let me know. The best by-product of screenwriting is that it blooms into the collaborative art of filmmaking and storytelling.

These are the stories I need to tell. Maybe we can tell some together.

In the first volume of this series, the stories were about powerful women. In volume two the focus is on men and the adventures and misadventures they often get themselves into. First up is *Vodka, a Vixen, and Vengeance in Vegas*, a rouge's romp through the casinos of Las Vegas and my attempt to combine elements of *The Hangover* with *Ocean's Eleven*. There are cons, crosses, double-crosses, mobsters, and of course a little seduction and sex—it is Vegas after all.

Geographically, *The Longest Subway Ride* could not be further removed from Las Vegas—nearly the entire film takes place in the factual and fictional world of the subway system of New York City. It is the story of one man, who, after making one fateful decision, ends up with a severe case of mistaken identity while exploring parts of the New York underground that most people would be surprised exists. It is one misadventure after another for our hero when all he wants to do is get to his original stop and back to the surface.

Douglas King
February 2020

LOGLINE

Seven half brothers meet for the first time upon learning of their con-artist father's death in Las Vegas, where they reluctantly partner with Russian mobsters in a con to avenge their father's murder by a powerful and ruthless casino owner.

Vodka, A Vixen, and Vengeance in Vegas

by
Douglas King

FADE IN

INT. CAR - DAY

Fraternal twins, DANIEL and PETE BACH, sit in a car outside
the Las Vegas Clark County Detention Center.

Daniel, short cropped hair, button-down shirt; looks like a
police officer, sits in the drivers seat.

Pete, much shorter, nerdy and insecure, fiddles with a tablet
computer while sitting in the passenger seat.

EXT. CLARK COUNTY DETENTION CENTER - SAME TIME

From the twin's POV - The front door to the Detention Center
opens and KELLY WOLFFE, a Calvin Klein fragrance model, steps
out. He dons designer sunglasses and looks both ways down the
street.

INT. CAR - SAME TIME

                    PETE
          Is that him?

                    DANIEL
          Your guess is as good as mine.

Daniel HONKS THE CAR HORN.

Kelly looks over at the car and Pete waves his hand out the
window.

Kelly approaches the vehicle.

                    KELLY
          Afternoon boys. I sure appreciate
          you picking me up.

                    PETE
          Least we could.

                    DANIEL
          Jump in. We're running late.

                    KELLY
          Amazing how little control you have
          over your schedule when you're in
          jail.

Kelly slides into the backseat and the car takes off down the street.

INT. FUNERAL HOME - DAY

FRANK RUSSELL, a handsome man in his fifties. He rests in a tuxedo, with just a hint of makeup covering his face.

He is dead.

Kelly, Daniel and Pete are three of five young men standing over the open casket.

Standing next to Kelly is HARRISON HOPE: nicely dressed, confident and TYCE ABRAMS: African-American, military hair-style and presence about him.

They are all brothers. Well...half-brothers.

ON FRANK

MONTAGE

-- LAS VEGAS CASINO -- Frank, about 37 years younger, sits at a blackjack table in a Las Vegas casino.

FREEZE FRAME on Frank. SUPER: "Frank Russell, 37 years ago, gambler, drinker, partier."

Frank is having a good time, laughing, drinking the free booze, and flirting with the waitress and the beautiful young BLACKJACK DEALER.

-- HOTEL SUITE -- Frank in bed with the blackjack dealer.

-- HOSPITAL -- Frank pacing in the waiting room of a hospital. A DOCTOR approaches him.

                    DOCTOR 1
          Congratulations, it's a boy.

-- PLUSH MANSION -- Frank, a few years older, at a party. He laughs, drinks and flirts with an ATTRACTIVE YOUNG WOMAN.

There is an obvious attraction.

They excuse themselves into a back bedroom away from the party.

-- HOSPITAL -- Frank pacing again in same hospital waiting room. The same Doctor approaches him.

> DOCTOR 1
> Congratulations, it's a boy.

-- COFFEE SHOP INSIDE A CASINO -- Frank, about 16 years older now, drinks coffee.

A YOUNG WAITRESS comes by to refill his coffee. She smiles.

He stops her and begins talking with her.

-- HOSPITAL -- Frank, once again paces in the waiting room of a hospital.

The doctor, approaches Frank.

> DOCTOR 1
> Congratulations Frank, it's twins.
> One is a bit scrawny, but both are
> healthy.

-- A BAR IN A SMALL CASINO -- Frank, older, looks a bit worse for wear. He drinks at the bar while a FLASHY SINGER sings in the background.

A not so attractive WORKING GIRL sits down next to Frank and asks if he would like to buy her a drink (MOS). He does.

-- HOSPITAL -- Frank pacing in a new hospital, not as nice as before. A young DOCTOR approaches him.

> DOCTOR 2
> Mr. Russell, you have a lovely baby
> boy.

BACK TO FUNERAL HOME

Daniel and Pete stare down at their father. Pete wipes a tear away. Daniel puts an arm around him.

Harrison watches this, shakes his head and walks away.

Kelly turns to watch Harrison leave.

INT. LAWYER'S OFFICE - DAY

All five brothers sit in a cramped office of a mid-level LAWYER.

It's obvious the office was not designed to hold six people, a desk, bookshelf and fake potted ficus plant.

The lawyer, old and tired, reads through the pages of the Will & Testament, there are only two.

>   LAWYER
>   This should be relatively simple.
>   Looks like Frank had nothing so
>   there is nothing to divide up.

Mumbling and grumbling from the group.

>   HARRISON
>   You couldn't have told us all this
>   on the phone and saved us a trip?

>   LAWYER
>   Well, your father did make this
>   video which he wanted you all to
>   see.

The lawyer pushes a few keys on his computer keyboard and spins the ancient CRT monitor around so the screen can be seen by the brothers.

The screen brightens and an image of Frank speaks directly to the viewer.

>   FRANK
>   Hello boys. I'm glad you're all
>   together. I'm sorry that the first
>   time you all meet had to be under
>   such circumstances. I really should
>   have tried to have a family reunion
>   or something.

When Frank says "family" he makes little quote symbols with his fingers.

>   FRANK (CONT'D)
>   I'm also sorry I wasn't a better
>   father to you boys. Listen, I tried
>   my best; as best as I knew how. For
>   some of you that simply meant
>   staying away. I knew you would do
>   better without me. But, I always
>   knew where you were and what you
>   were doing and if you or your mom
>   ever needed anything I did my best
>   to provide. Okay, bottom line boys,
>   if you're watching this, then I'm
>   dead. Murdered to be precise. I
>   know, I know. You're probably
>   thinking, who would want to kill a
>   great guy like me, but trust me,
>   someone did. Not that there is a
>   long list of suspects.
>   (MORE)

                    LAWYER
          This should be relatively simple.
          Looks like Frank had nothing so
          there is nothing to divide up.

Mumbling and grumbling from the group.

                    HARRISON
          You couldn't have told us all this
          on the phone and saved us a trip?

                    LAWYER
          Well, your father did make this
          video which he wanted you all to
          see.

The lawyer pushes a few keys on his computer keyboard and
spins the ancient CRT monitor around so the screen can be
seen by the brothers.

The screen brightens and an image of Frank speaks directly to
the viewer.

                    FRANK
          Hello boys. I'm glad you're all
          together. I'm sorry that the first
          time you all meet had to be under
          such circumstances. I really should
          have tried to have a family reunion
          or something.

When Frank says "family" he makes little quote symbols with
his fingers.

                    FRANK (CONT'D)
          I'm also sorry I wasn't a better
          father to you boys. Listen, I tried
          my best; as best as I knew how. For
          some of you that simply meant
          staying away. I knew you would do
          better without me. But, I always
          knew where you were and what you
          were doing and if you or your mom
          ever needed anything I did my best
          to provide. Okay, bottom line boys,
          if you're watching this, then I'm
          dead. Murdered to be precise. I
          know, I know. You're probably
          thinking, who would want to kill a
          great guy like me, but trust me,
          someone did. Not that there is a
          long list of suspects.
                    (MORE)

                    FRANK (CONT'D)
          I pride myself on having more
          friends than enemies, but obviously
          it only takes one and I am asking
          you boys, my boys, to avenge me.

                    HARRISON
          Give me a freaking break!

                    PETE
          Shhhh!

                    FRANK
          Some of you are probably asking,
          "Why would you want to avenge a
          father you never really knew?"

                    HARRISON
          You've got that right.

Kelly stares at Harrison.

                    FRANK
          Because it's the right thing to do.
          Listen, I was murdered. You're my
          family and I'm asking you to right
          the wrongs that have been done
          here. Help set my spirit free.

                    HARRISON
          Oh man.

                    FRANK
          The most likely suspect is Raleigh
          Bonner.

INT. CASINO - DAY

FREEZE FRAME on RALEIGH as he exits elevator. SUPER: "Raleigh
Bonner, owner of The Palace, general thug."

Raleigh is all flash and no bang. The type of guy who walks
with a decorative walking cane, though he doesn't need it.
The definition for "poser" shows Raleigh's picture.

As the action starts again, Raleigh walks through his casino.

Following closely behind him is a mountain of a man (if one
can call a 300 pound brute, a man), GEOFFREY, Raleigh's
personal security.

                    FRANK (V.O.)
          Raleigh owns The Palace, a
          hotel/casino on the south end of
          the Strip. He desperately dreams of
          being in the big league with the
          likes of Wynn, Adelson, and Trump.
          I was helping him get there with a
          killer new concept I came up with.
          We tied on-line gambling with a
          physical casino. On-line gaming is
          going to rescue the brick and
          mortar casino biz when congress
          passes the Barney Frank bill.
          Raleigh is making sure that happens
          by greasing a few politician palms.
          With my idea and his politicians we
          couldn't lose. Wynn tried to buy my
          idea but Raleigh offered me a
          partnership. My idea was genius. I
          was about to apply for a patent
          that would protect my idea, but...
          If I'm dead, that means he stole my
          idea and wanted to cut me out,
          keeping it all for himself. You
          can't let him get away with it
          boys. Okay, I got to go, I can't
          keep Saint Peter waiting. I love
          you all.

BACK TO THE LAWYER'S OFFICE

The video stops and the lawyer spins the monitor around to
face him again.

                    LAWYER
          I guess that covers it. Any
          questions?

EXT. POOL SIDE AT THE MIRAGE - DAY

The brothers sit around a table looking like a lost litter of
puppies.

Tyce nurses a cocktail.

Pete has a laptop with him.

Harrison texts on his phone.

Kelly scans the pool for attractive, interested women.

                         PETE
               You know, dad's idea was actually
               brilliant. It offered a two-value
               cash out for the player which will
               revolutionize the industry.

                         HARRISON
               First, can we not call him dad?
               Second, using the word brilliant to
               describe anything he did is a
               stretch.

Pete reacts. Shot down like a nerd on ladies night at a bar.

Harrison stands.

                         HARRISON
               Well guys, its been great meeting
               you all. I would love to stay and
               bond, but I have a business to get
               back to in LA.

                         KELLY
               What type?

                         HARRISON
                    (hesitant to say)
               I run an event planning company. We
               set up parties, dinners, functions
               for Fortune 500 companies,
               celebrities, award shows.

                         KELLY
               Very cool.

The other brothers nod their agreement.

                         HARRISON
               Thanks. Yeah well, like I said...

                         KELLY
               C'mon dude, you can't just bail.
               Our father was murdered...

                         HARRISON
               Seriously? Just cause Frank says
               something on a video that was made
               who knows when, doesn't mean it's
               true. This guy was a player and a
               con man.

                         PETE
               He was also our dad.

Nobody says anything until Harrison breaks the silence.

                    HARRISON
          Look guys, Frank may have been the
          sperm donor for each of us, but he
          was never a father to any of us. I
          am not going to be part of anything
          illegal.

                    KELLY
          Who said anything about illegal?

                    TYCE
          Yeah, I don't see the point either.

                    DANIEL
          I'm planning to join the police
          academy soon. I don't need anything
          screwing that up.

                    PETE
          C'mon, bro!

                    DANIEL
          You c'mon. You know what that means
          to me.

                    PETE
          But --

                    KELLY
          What better way to prove yourself
          than to solve your own father's
          murder?

                    HARRISON
          Are you that twisted that you would
          risk his career so you can get
          revenge for some guy you barely
          knew? Frank was probably killed by
          some jealous husband for shagging
          his wife. The police can deal with
          it.

The brothers sit in silence for a minute.

                    KELLY
          Or, what he said was true and he
          invented something that could
          change the face of gambling. If so,
          that invention is rightfully ours.
          Aren't you the least bit curious to
          know the truth?

Harrison shrugs.

                    KELLY (CONT'D)
          C'mon!

               TYCE
          That is a bit cold man.

               HARRISON
          You just said --

               TYCE
          I know what I said. That was before
          I knew there was a possible
          inheritance.

               PETE
          I did a little digging around the
          police records about dad's death
          and learned they found his body
          behind Planet Hollywood. He had a
          high blood alcohol content so I
          figure he was drinking in Privé.

               HARRISON
          Figures.

               PETE
          Why don't we talk to someone over
          there and see if they know
          anything.

               KELLY
          How did you find this out?

               PETE
          It's amazing what you can learn on
          the Internet -- If you know where
          to look.
               (beat)
          I hacked the police report.

               KELLY
          Way to go, bro.
               (to group)
          That sounds good to me.

               HARRISON
          And then what?

               KELLY
      We'll know once we know more. All
      we're doing is asking a few
      questions. No big deal. Right,
      Daniel?

Daniel nods.

               DANIEL
      I guess.

Collectively the group nods. Harrison just stares at his
phone.

INT. PRIVÉ - NIGHT

Kelly and Pete stand inside Privé, a loud nightclub and bar
located at the Planet Hollywood Resort and Casino. They talk
with the BOUNCER at the front entrance.

Actually they are shouting, because the music is so loud.

               BOUNCER
      Yeah, I remember Frank. Good guy.

               KELLY
      Were you here the night he was
      murdered?

The Bouncer grimaces. Uncomfortable. Looks around to see
who's watching.

               BOUNCER
      Yeah.

               KELLY
      Can you tell us anything you
      remember from that night?

               BOUNCER
      Let's see. He came in kinda
      early...

               KELLY
      Alone?

A group of attractive young ladies walk past and the bouncer
lets them into the club.

Kelly checks them out, while Pete stares at them long after
they have entered the club. He is in love. Lust.

                    BOUNCER
          Yeah. Came in alone but it didn't
          take long before he had a young
          lady. In fact...

FLASHBACK -- INT. PRIVE - NIGHT

Frank sits at the bar talking with JULIETTE MICHAELS, the
type of woman wars are fought over.

They sit away from the rest of the crowd and lean very close
to each other to be heard over the noise.

Geoffrey approaches them and grabs Juliette by her elbow.

When Frank tries to stop Geoffrey, which was a stupid thing
to do, he is shoved to the floor unceremoniously.

                    FRANK
          Leave her alone Geoffrey.

                    GEOFFREY
          I'm not here for her Frank...I'm
          here for you. But, she needs to
          come too.

Frank stands up to face Geoffrey again. The second stupid
thing Frank has done.

Geoffrey grabs Frank with his free hand, pinning Franks's arm
behind his back, while still restraining Juliette with his
other -- this guy really is a huge beast.

Geoffrey escorts both Frank and Juliette out of the club past
the bouncer.

BACK TO SCENE

                    BOUNCER
          That was the last I saw him until
          the cops showed up.

                    KELLY
          Did you recognize the girl or the
          guy?

                    BOUNCER
          Sure. The girl was Raleigh Bonner's
          girl, Juliette, and the guy was
          Raleigh's bodyguard.

Kelly looks at Pete like he found the missing piece of the
puzzle.

                    KELLY
          Thanks.
              (to Pete)
          Give him a little somethin'
          somethin', ya know.

                    PETE
          Why you looking at me for that?

                    KELLY
          Because I haven't had time to hit
          an ATM. Now tip the man from your
          titty bar stash, will ya, and meet
          me outside.

Pete looks at the bouncer who has been listening to their
exchange.

                    PETE
              (meekly)
          Are one's okay?

INT. THE PALACE - CASINO FLOOR - DAY

Golden elevator doors open and Geoffrey exits. Hidden behind
him is Raleigh and Juliette, Raleigh's arm candy. A kept
woman.

As Raleigh exits the elevator, an elderly couple -- guests of
his hotel -- step in front of him, nearly bumping into him.

                    RALEIGH
          Excuse me! Do you see me walking
          here? Well, do you? I mean come on.
          When an elevator opens do you just
          dash willy nilly into it? Or would
          the polite thing be to wait for the
          people inside to exit and then you
          enter? Yes, I think that would be
          best, wouldn't it? Shall we try
          that again then?

The couple do not know what to do, step aside or step into
the elevator.

Raleigh grows more exasperated.

                    RALEIGH (CONT'D)
          Gaaa, you really are thick-headed
          aren't you? Make sure to gamble a
          lot... Cheers.
              (under his breath)

Raleigh brushes past the couple and leaves them standing there wondering what just happened.

The trio walk on through the casino.

> RALEIGH
> Really, Geoffrey, it is your job to see to it that those type of things don't happen, isn't it?

Geoffrey nods.

> RALEIGH (CONT'D)
> I shouldn't have to put up with the masses like that. Do you think Steve Wynn nearly gets bowled over when he exits his own elevator? No, of course not. He shields himself from the riff raff, doesn't he?

Geoffrey nods again.

> JULIETTE
> Raleigh?

> RALEIGH
> Yes, dear.

> JULIETTE
> You won't be needing me today will you? I was hoping to go do some shopping.

> RALEIGH
> (sarcastically)
> Right, run along and spend more money. I am sorry that you only have seventy-two pair of shoes. I know that is a terrible imposition on you.

> JULIETTE
> Actually, I was going to look for something for you, but now...

> RALEIGH
> I'm sorry, love. I'm just in a foul mood now. Have a good time. You need anything? Black Amex?

> JULIETTE
> I'm good, thanks. Just try to be in a good mood when I return.

Raleigh smiles and leans in for a kiss. Juliette complies but it is apparent that she does so reluctantly. Juliette exits.

Geoffrey leads the way for Raleigh, clearing people out of their path like a snow plow as they move through the casino.

Daniel and Pete sit at a nearby gaming table. The pair have been watching and listening.

Daniel throws a tip to the DEALER and the brothers follow Raleigh.

EXT. LUXURY CONDO - LATER

Raleigh's limo stops in front of a luxury condo.

Geoffrey steps out of the front seat passenger side, comes around the car and opens the door for Raleigh.

They both enter the building.

A minute later Daniel and Pete drive passed. Pete writes down the address.

As they drive away they pass a large BILLBOARD promoting The Palace casino and its upcoming poker tournament.

INT. THE BOULEVARD - DAY

Juliette walks through The Boulevard shopping center.

She has a few bags on her arms.

Kelly follows Juliette at a safe distance. He tails her, which isn't a bad task considering how beautiful and attractively dressed she is. Two facts Kelly has certainly noticed.

Juliette enters another high-end store.

Kelly stops at a bench outside the store and begins texting on his phone -- at least giving the impression he is.

Juliette exits the store just moments after she entered and walks straight up to Kelly.

She sits down on the bench next to him, placing her bags between him and her.

                         JULIETTE
              So...do I need to call security and
              tell them I have a stalker, or are
              you going to tell me who hired you
              to follow me?

Kelly is shocked at the accusation.

                         KELLY
              What? Who me?

                         JULIETTE
              Don't play stupid. You've been
              tailing me since I left Victoria's
              Secret. That fact alone makes you
              creepy, but I am willing to give
              you the benefit of the doubt that
              it was just a coincidence.

                         KELLY
              That was a very nice bra you
              purchased.

                         JULIETTE
              Okay, security it is.

Juliette begins to stand.

                         KELLY
              No wait. My name's Kelly Wolffe.

He reaches out to shake her hand. She thinks about it then
shakes.

                         JULIETTE
              What do you do Mr. Wolffe? Trying
              to get me to tell you the location
              of grandmother's house?

                         KELLY
              Clever. Smart and beautiful that is
              a rare combination.

                         JULIETTE
              You didn't answer my question.

                         KELLY
              Real estate. Buy and sell. How
              about you?

                         JULIETTE
              I buy. Clothes, bags, make up.

                    KELLY
          Must be nice.

                    JULIETTE
          Well, this has been a pleasant
          conversation, but I think the
          mental stimulation has been enough
          for me for one day.

Juliette smiles and rises from the bench.

                    KELLY
          Does the name Frank Russell mean
          anything to you?

                    JULIETTE
          I'm beginning to suspect this
          wasn't a chance meeting?

                    KELLY
          It wasn't.

Juliette turns to leave. Kelly stands to follow.

                    JULIETTE
          Don't follow me. Don't touch me.
          Don't talk to me.

                    KELLY
          Frank Russell was my father.

Juliette stops.

                    KELLY (CONT'D)
          I need some information to confirm
          something I believe I already know.
          You are the only one who can
          definitively help me.

Juliette turns to face Kelly.

                    JULIETTE
          And why would I want to do that?

                    KELLY
          I'm hoping that you hate Raleigh
          Bonner as much as I do. I know you
          are his girl and--

                    JULIETTE
          I'm not...

                         KELLY
          Whatever. It's none of my business
          why you stay with him, but --

                         JULIETTE
          You have no idea what he's capable
          of.

                         KELLY
          I have a clue.

                         JULIETTE
          No. What he did to your dad, that
          was merciful compared to what he
          has done to others.

                         KELLY
          Is that why you stay?

                         JULIETTE
          The last girl who left Raleigh,
          took a nose dive from the Ghost Bar
          at the Palm. Happened on a Friday
          night when the bar was full and yet
          no one saw a thing. How do you
          think that happened?

                         KELLY
          So the guy has rejection issues.

                         JULIETTE
          That's putting it mildly. How about
          control issues, sexual issues,
          mother issues, and more? He has
          more issues than National
          Geographic.

                         KELLY
          Tell me what you remember about the
          night Frank was murdered.

Juliette looks away, a sad and frightened look on her face,
as she remembers...

FLASHBACK -- EXT. PLANET HOLLYWOOD - LOADING DOCK - NIGHT

Scene is a continuation from page 13.

Geoffrey has Juliette and Frank, one in each hand, leading
them to a limousine idling near a trash can behind Planet
Hollywood.

Raleigh steps out from the back seat and motions for Juliette to get in.

Silently, she does.

> FRANK
> Juliette, you don't...

Frank's thoughts are interrupted by Geoffrey's fist in his stomach causing Frank's brain to momentarily forget what he was going to say and focus entirely on getting air back into his lungs.

He falls to his knees in the hope that will help.

> RALEIGH
> Frank, you are a smart guy, did you really think I was so dumb that I wouldn't know what you were doing?

> FRANK
> It's not like that, Raleigh.

> RALEIGH
> I know what it is. I've been having you followed for awhile now. You can't lie to me, Frank.

> FRANK
> Raleigh c'mon, I wouldn't...

> RALEIGH
> I know about your little double deal?

> FRANK
> What?

Raleigh nods to Geoffrey and he punches Frank in the stomach again.

> RALEIGH
> Did you really think you could sell
> *my* program to another buyer?

> FRANK
> Raleigh, I'm not. I was trying to get us the cash to finish. I knew things were tight with the bank.

> RALEIGH
> You don't know anything, Frank.
>> (beat)
>> (MORE)

                    RALEIGH (CONT'D)
You know this actually works out
really well. See I was starting to
rethink our little arrangement--

                    FRANK
But Raleigh the program was my
idea. I've got the patent ready to
go.

                    RALEIGH
Yeah but you haven't sent it yet
have you? So really who's to say
who came up with it? I tell you
what I'm going to do. Since I like
you...well... we were once
partners, I'm not going to have
Geoffrey rough you up any more.

                    FRANK
Thank you.

                    RALEIGH
You're welcome. Instead I'm going
to have him kill you.
        (beat)
Geoffrey, kill him.

Juliette steps out of the car to scream for Frank.

                    JULIETTE
    Frank!

Raleigh backhands Juliette and she slumps into the backseat.

                    RALEIGH
    Stay in the car!

Geoffrey executes Frank where he is kneeling. His lifeless
body slumps to the ground.

                    RALEIGH
Brilliant. I was thinking you might
take him somewhere more discreet.

                    GEOFFREY
    Oh.

                    RALEIGH
Yeah. Thinking isn't a strong suit
for you is it, Geoffrey? Remind me
to put in a raise for you next
check.

                         GEOFFREY
                 Thanks boss.

                         RALEIGH
                 No...I was being sarcass...oh never
                 mind. What's done is done. Leave
                 the body. Get in the car.

BACK TO SCENE

                         JULIETTE
                 There was nothing I could do.

                         KELLY
                 I know.
                         (beat)
                 But now you can. I need your help.

INT. DENNY'S - DAY

The brothers sit in the largest booth Denny's has.

                         KELLY
                 I believe we can take Raleigh down.
                 We're going to need to pool our
                 talents.

                         PETE
                 I can hack any site you want.

                         KELLY
                 Excellent.

                         TYCE
                 The military taught me surveillance
                 skills, among other things.

Kelly looks at Tyce a little concerned and cautiously.

                         KELLY
                 That will come in handy. Daniel,
                 you can be the muscle and security.
                 Pete and Tyce we are also going to
                 need some false identities. Can you
                 handle that?

                         PETE
                 Sure, you know where people are
                 going to look for things and you
                 simply add what you need.

                    KELLY
          We will need some back stories for
          Harrison and me.

                    HARRISON
          Wait a minute...

                    PETE
          This is so cool. It will be like
          Ocean's Eleven, only there are five
          of us. We can be Kelly's Five.

                    TYCE
          How about Kelly's Heroes?

                    DANIEL
          That was a great movie. Clint
          Eastwood was awesome.

                    HARRISON
          Guys! I thought you were just
          asking questions? Suddenly you have
          a plan?

                    KELLY
          Asked and answered. We have the
          evidence.

                    HARRISON
          The word of a bouncer and a call
          girl.

                    KELLY
          She's not a call girl! She's
          Raleigh's girlfriend. Frank knew
          her.

                    HARRISON
          I bet he did. Daniel, you can't be
          cool with this?

                    DANIEL
          I haven't heard the plan yet.

                    HARRISON
          Are you going to listen to a guy we
          just picked up from jail to plan a
          con to help a dead guy we barely
          knew?

The table sits in silence.

                    PETE
          I'm good. You guys?

Pete looks around the table pleadingly.

                    TYCE
          I don't have anything better to do.

Harrison rolls his eyes in exasperation as each brother
agrees to be part of Kelly's plan.

                    DANIEL
          I won't do anything illegal.

                    KELLY
          We won't tell you about the illegal
          stuff.

INT. RALEIGH BONNER'S OFFICE -DAY

Raleigh's office is decorated as if time stood still from the
inception of Las Vegas. If memories could bring back a time
long gone, this office would do it.

NEOGOD69, someone who never leaves his computer and exists
solely on Mountain Dew and Cheetos sits in front of Raleigh.

He demonstrates the latest build of the program he is coding
for him.

A large screen mounted on the wall shows the software in
action.

Raleigh tries to follow along with what the program can do.

Geoffrey sits on a couch reading a magazine.

Juliette files her nails and stares out the large picture
window that looks out over downtown Las Vegas. Occasionally,
she looks up to watch the monitor.

                    KELLY (V.O.)
          Raleigh is leveraged up the ass. He
          owes the bank millions and is
          losing as much each month on his
          casino. With the big development
          boom focused on the north end of
          the strip, Raleigh is eager and
          desperate to bring people back
          south.

                    DANIEL (V.O.)
          I read that downtown casino
          winnings are off seven percent.

                    KELLY (V.O.)
          I'm sure. And that's not all. With
          the new Cosmopolitan and CityCenter
          opening, more than 6,000 new rooms
          opened smack in the middle of the
          strip and most are empty. Even
          beating-off is in recession. In-
          room porn on demand has dropped
          twenty-three percent. Frank knew
          all this and that is why he was
          developing this new on-line gaming
          software. He hired some hotshot
          programmer and was having the thing
          written to his specs. He also knew
          the bank would no longer loan
          Raleigh the cash needed to renovate
          and operate the casino let alone a
          new online project. That's when
          Frank started looking elsewhere for
          funding, only Raleigh thought Frank
          was going to double cross him,
          because Frank had started sleeping
          with Raleigh's girlfriend.

INT. DENNY'S - DAY

                    HARRISON
          Figures.

                    KELLY
          The software is nearly finished,
          but the programmer won't give it to
          Raleigh until he's paid in full.
          So...we're going to buy it.

                    HARRISON
          Where are we going to get the
          money?

INT. LUXURY CONDO - NIGHT

Neogod69 sits at his state of the art computer terminal
typing code.

Kelly and Daniel, dressed in finely tailored suits, stand
behind him.

                    KELLY (V.O.)
          Technically we won't be buying
          anything, but we need to give the
          appearance that we are.

                    HARRISON (V.O.)
          Meaning?

                    KELLY (V.O.)
          That's your play. We're going to
          set you up as a new buyer with
          backing from Macau. You're going to
          outbid Raleigh for the program.
               (beat)
          Ty, I need you to set up a way for
          us to remotely steal the code and
          keep tabs on the programmer.

                    TYCE (V.O.)
          Easy. Done.

Daniel places a computer bug near Neogod69's computers.

                    KELLY (V.O.)
          Once we get the software, Pete, I
          need you to duplicate it but put a
          few bugs in it.

INT. HOTEL SUITE - NIGHT

Pete sits with his laptop typing code.

When he finishes, he pulls a flash drive from his computer
and hands it to Harrison.

                    PETE
          No prob.

INT. DENNY'S - DAY

                    KELLY
          Finally, Raleigh needs money. He's
          going to need to reach out to
          someone. That's where the Russians
          come in.

                    HARRISON
          Wait. Who?

INT. RALEIGH BONNER'S OFFICE -DAY

Neogod69 leaves Raleigh's office, escorted by Geoffrey.

When Geoffrey returns he sits down across from Raleigh.

                    RALEIGH
          That little wanker thinks he can
          hold out on me? Who's he to make
          demands? When we have the code I
          want you to put two in the back of
          his skull. Got it?

                    GEOFFREY
          Yes.

                    RALEIGH
          Good. Oh, and this time do it
          somewhere discreet like say the
          hundreds of miles of desert that
          surround us.

Geoffrey nods.

Raleigh reaches for his phone and dials.

As the phone connects the SCREEN SLIDES OVER.

The phone is answered by BRUCE DURGAN.

INT. DURGAN'S OFFICE

Durgan's office looks like the Romanov family decorator threw
up after an orgy.

The THUMP THUMP of LOUD CLUB MUSIC is MUFFLED background
music.

Bruce makes 1980s *Miami Vice* fashion and style still look
cool.

FREEZE FRAME ON BRUCE. SUPER: "Bruce Durgan, consigliere for
the Russian mafia."

SPLIT SCREEN

ON THE LEFT - RALEIGH'S OFFICE

ON THE RIGHT - DURGAN'S OFFICE

                    BRUCE
          Hello?

                    RALEIGH
          Bruce?

                    BRUCE
Speaking. Who's this?

                    RALEIGH
Raleigh Bonner. I own The Palace.

                    BRUCE
Okay.

                    RALEIGH
Right.

                    BRUCE
What can I do you for, Raleigh?

                    RALEIGH
I need to make arrangements for a
loan.

                    BRUCE
We're not a bank.

                    RALEIGH
Of course.

                    BRUCE
I assume you know our terms?

                    RALEIGH
I have heard.

                    BRUCE
Then, let me see what I can do. May
take a day or two.

                    RALEIGH
Is that necessary? Can't we
schedule...

                    BRUCE
Yes, Raleigh it is necessary. This
is how we do things. You want to be
involved with us then you wait for
a call back. First we do a
background check and make sure
everything is copacetic. I'm going
to assume that the very fact you
are calling us means you can't go
anywhere else, so let's play by the
rules and see if we can get you
what you want.

Raleigh is not used to be spoken to in this manner.

                    RALEIGH
          Right. I understand.

                    BRUCE
          Good. I'm sure we'll be in touch.
               (beat)
          Relax, Raleigh. You sound really
          uptight.

Bruce hangs up the phone.

SPLIT SCREEN ENDS

INT. OFFICE - FBI HEADQUARTERS - DAY

Sitting in a dimly lit room is FBI agent GREG GARCIA. A
career agent.

FREEZE FRAME. SUPER: "Greg Garcia, FBI agent."

The room is filled with surveillance equipment.

The door to the office opens and JD HILL, another agent,
enters.

FREEZE FRAME. SUPER: "JD HILL, FBI agent in charge of special
operations."

                    JD
          What's up?

                    GREG
          Raleigh Bonner just contacted our
          Russians for a loan. May be
          something, may not.

                    JD
          Bonner, the casino owner? British?

                    GREG
          Yeah.

                    JD
          I'd say that's something.

INT. THE PALAZZO - CHECK IN DESK - DAY

Kelly speaks with an attractive, well dressed, professional
woman, the FRONT DESK MANAGER.

Pete stands next to Kelly, observing.

As she hands Kelly the electronic key she winks.

                    DAY MANAGER
          I think you will find this suite to
          your liking sir. Please let me know
          if there is anything I can be of
          further assistance with.

                    KELLY
          You know I will. Thank you very
          much for all of your help.

Kelly turns to walk away then turns back.

                    KELLY (CONT'D)
          How's the new home?

                    DAY MANAGER
          Absolutely perfect.

                    KELLY
          I knew it would be.

                    DAY MANAGER
          We're even now?

                    KELLY
          Square as four ninety degree
          angles.

Kelly smiles and walks away.

INT. LUXURY CONDO - DAY

If Mark Zuckerberg were an interior designer, he most likely
would have designed a home to look like this.

One of the few pieces of furniture is a desk lined with flat
panel monitors and external hard drives.

Harrison, posing as Thurston, an employee for a Chinese
casino owner from Macau, stands in the condo.

Backing him up is Daniel.

Neogod69 sits at his desk sipping an energy drink, empty cans
of which are strewn across the floor.

                    NEOGOD69
          You know I checked you out Mr.
          Thurston and I found nothing.

                    HARRISON
          Does that surprise you? What'd you
          expect a freaking Wikipedia page?
          The people I work for and the
          things I do, well, let's just say
          we don't like a lot of notoriety.

                    NEOGOD69
          Yeah well...

                    HARRISON
          Listen kid, if you don't want our
          money, I'll find someone else to
          give it to.

                    NEOGOD69
          There is no one who can code the
          way I do. This program is solid.

                    HARRISON
          I'm glad your ego is big, I wish
          you mouth wasn't.

INT. THE PALAZZO - SUITE - SAME TIME

The suite has become the brothers 'war room.'

Tyce and Pete sit in front of a bank of flat panel computer
screens. They listen to the conversation between Harrison and
Neogod69.

                    PETE
          Give me a break. Whose this kid
          think he is?

                    TYCE
          Don't get your undies in a wad --

                    PETE
          No one can code the way he does.
          That's wack. Wait 'til he sees my
          mad code.

                    TYCE
          Please don't so that.

                    PETE
          What?

                    TYCE
          Try to talk black. It's ugly on
          you.

                    PETE
          But --

                    TYCE
          No. Just wrong.

BACK TO LUXURY CONDO

                    NEOGOD69
          So you have the cash to buy the
          program?

                    HARRISON
          I do. I can wire the money--

                    NEOGOD69
          No way man. I'm old school when it
          comes to money. I only do cash. I
          don't trust the banking system. You
          know how easily it can be hacked?

                    HARRISON
          Okay.
               (beat)
          When will the program be ready?

While Harrison has engaged Neogod69 in the conversation
Daniel slips a small device out of his pocket and tries to
covertly place it near the computers.

                    NEOGOD69
          Two days tops.

                    HARRISON
          Good. I will want to see a demo
          first, of course.

                    NEOGOD69
          No problem.

Neogod69 notices Daniel edging closer to his desk and
computers.

                    NEOGOD69 (CONT'D)
          Hey man back your junk up. This
          ain't no Best Buy. You don't get to
          test the equipment.

Harrison tries to distract Neogod69.

                    HARRISON
          Relax. He won't touch anything.
          Besides I don't think you want my
          man to touch you either.

Daniel steps forward to threaten Neogod69 who backs down
quickly.

                    NEOGOD69
          Chill. I'm chill. I just get
          protective about my rig.

Daniel successfully attaches the device near the computers
and motions to Harrison.

                    HARRISON
          Just focus on your work. With this
          payday you can buy yourself a whole
          new rig. I will call you in two
          days.

INT. THE PALAZZO - SUITE - LATER

Pete and Tyce each click away on their own laptop.

One screen shows security footage from the The Palace Casino
and Hotel.

                    TYCE
          How you coming along?

                    PETE
          Hotel security feed up. Thank God
          for the new cloud computing. Makes
          hacking much easier. What about
          you?

                    TYCE
          All systems go. The bug is working.
          I'll send you the patch so you can
          begin to download.

                    PETE
          We are good, dawg. We be all
          gangster.

                    TYCE
          I told you, don't do that.

                    PETE
          Sure, sure, okay.
               (beat)
                              (MORE)

                    PETE (CONT'D)
          So how'd you learn to do all of
          this stuff anyway?

                    TYCE
          The military taught me a lot about
          computers, but it was Frank who got
          me interested even before that.

                    PETE
          Really?

INT. LIBRARY - DAY

FLASHBACK - Frank sits with a teenage Tyce in front of a
computer.

                    FRANK
          Anything you want to know is on the
          Internet Ty, you just have to know
          where to look and how to look. Me,
          I know enough to download porn,
          catch a virus, or both, but I'm not
          smart enough to know how to hack
          into some place that doesn't want
          me in, and therein lies the real
          power. That's like gold.

Tyce looks up at his dad and smiles.

INT. CHURCH - DAY

Harrison sits in the pew of a small church. His eyes closed
in prayer.

Kelly enters and quietly sits down next to him.

Eventually Harrison opens his eyes and looks at Kelly.

                    KELLY
          I didn't want to disturb you.

                    HARRISON
          I appreciate that.

                    KELLY
          You looked rather peaceful.

                    HARRISON
          Probably the most I've been since
          this crazy week started. Prayer
          does that for me. Helps me to focus
          on what is really important.

                    KELLY
          So what's important?

                    HARRISON
          Honestly it's my business and
          family back home, but then you guys
          are my family now too, and I guess
          in a way -- though I hate to admit
          it -- so is Frank.

The two sit in silence for a beat.

                    KELLY
          Do you have any memories of Frank?

                    HARRISON
          A few.

                    KELLY
          Any good ones?

                    HARRISON
          There was one time he came out to
          see me and my mom in California.

FLASHBACK -- EXT. DEL MAR RACE TRACK - DAY

Frank sits with a ten year old Harrison in the stands of a
race track watching the horses.

                    FRANK
          Son, the way you pick horses is
          really very simple. Sure you have
          to look at the jockey, track
          conditions and all of that, but
          focus on the bloodline.
          Thoroughbred horses were actually
          developed in the 18th century. Cool
          huh?

The young Harrison nods his head.

                    FRANK (CONT'D)
          English owners bred their mares
          with Arabian stallions in order to
          create a better breed of horse for
          running great distances. All
          thoroughbreds are descendants of
          three horses: the Darley Arabian,
          the Godolphin Arabian, and the
          Byerly Turk. Racetrack earnings can
          all be traced back and matched to
          specific studs.
                    (MORE)

                         FRANK (CONT'D)
                    The greater the earnings the
                    greater the stud fees will be.
                    Bloodlines from Storm Cat and
                    Troienne are incredible, and the
                    earnings from those horses are in
                    the millions. Always look at the
                    bloodline, that is the key.

Just then the horses for the current race turn the final
corner and race to the finish line.

Franks stands and cheers his horse on.

Young Harrison watches with excitement. <u>He is as happy to be
with his dad, as he is to see if his horse will win.</u>

When the horses reach the finish line Frank cheers. <u>Their
horse won.</u>

                         FRANK (CONT'D)
                    We did it son! We won! What did I
                    tell you? Always trust the
                    bloodline.

BACK TO SCENE

                         KELLY
                    You and I have kind of been at odds
                    since we meet. I think we're both
                    alpha males looking to see who's
                    going to lead.

                         HARRISON
                    Kelly you're asking me to
                    participate in something I don't
                    believe in --

                         KELLY
                    -- but you could.

                         HARRISON
                    -- don't trust.

                         KELLY
                    -- but you will.

                         HARRISON
                    -- and don't completely understand.

                         KELLY
                    Ah, there in lies the rub.

                    HARRISON
I'm not like you Kelly. I don't see
the world as one big opportunity
waiting for me to snatch it. I've
had to work hard for everything I
have.

                    KELLY
You don't think I've worked hard?

                    HARRISON
This week has been mind blowing to
say the least. One day I'm an only
child to a father I never really
knew, the next, I'm one of the
oldest brothers to a group that
reminds me of the cast from the Bad
News Bears.

                    KELLY
Now that was a classic. The
original with Walter Matthau. Which
character am I?

                    HARRISON
I think it is only appropriate that
you be the Kelly Leak character.

                    KELLY
Does that make you Tanner, or the
one played by Tatum O'Neal?

                    HARRISON
Nice.

                    KELLY
Listen man. It's weird for all of
us but we might as well embrace it.
I think it's pretty cool I have
four baby bros now.

                    HARRISON
Sure, it increases your odds of
making bail.

                    KELLY
There is that.

                    HARRISON
I just need to get my head around
this.
                    (MORE)

                    HARRISON (CONT'D)
          You're asking me -- all of us -- to
          take part in something we have no
          experience doing, no expertise in,
          and for some of us, flies in the
          face of who we are.

                    KELLY
          But, aside from that --

                    HARRISON
          -- it's a great plan.

                    KELLY
          What happened to Frank was wrong.
          Even if he was the world's greatest
          douche bag --

                    HARRISON
          -- which he was.

                    KELLY
          He still didn't deserve what
          happened to him, and there's no one
          else that can make sure that the
          guy who did this gets what he
          deserves.

INT. FBI HEADQUARTERS - DAY

Agents Greg and JD sit in their office comparing notes.

Photos of Bruce and his Russian associates line one wall, and
photos of Raleigh and Geoffrey have been tacked up along side
them.

                    GREG
          So we put some men on watching
          Raleigh once he reached out to the
          Russians. So far nothing unusual.

                    JD
          Stay with it. Raleigh's a powerful
          man to be associating with these
          criminals. Something is going down.

                    GREG
          I'm putting a couple of men UC for
          this upcoming tournament that
          Raleigh is holding. I figure maybe
          this has something to do with that.

                    JD
          Could be. Play it out and let's see
          what comes of it.

INT. THE PALAZZO - SUITE - NIGHT

Kelly and Harrison enter.

Daniel watches everything Pete and Tyce do.

                    HARRISON
          I have to admit this is impressive.

                    PETE
          Yeah, this place is pimped out.

                    TYCE
          What did I tell you about trying to
          be all gangster?

                    PETE
          Oh yeah, sorry.

                    HARRISON
          This is going to look suspicious to
          house cleaning.

                    KELLY
          Don't worry. I have everything
          under control.
               (beat)
          All right boys, how's everything
          coming along?

                    TYCE
          Good. All we need now are eyes in
          Raleigh's office so we can track
          his moves and we should have all
          the bases covered.

                    KELLY
          Working on that.

Not to be outdone.

                    PETE
          Well, I have nearly cracked Neo's
          security...the kid is good.

                    TYCE
          Kid? You're calling him a kid?

                    PETE
          C'mon. I'm at least two years older
          than him.

                    KELLY
          Anyway...?

                    PETE
          I should be finished tonight.

                    KELLY
          Great job Petey. Who da man? You da
          man!

Kelly does a fist bump with Pete. Pete revels in the
attention.

INT. RALEIGH BONNER'S OFFICE - EARLY MORNING

Raleigh's office is dark. The only illumination comes from
the neon glow of the Vegas strip.

A shadowy figure moves through the office.

As the figure passes in front of the windows a clear female
silhouette is cut -- Juliette.

She makes her way to Raleigh's desk and places a tiny camera
on the desk where it is hidden and will not be noticed.

She repeats this move a few times throughout the office,
placing small cameras in places that provide the best
coverage but will go unnoticed.

A noise outside the office startles her and she stops and
waits to see what it is.

She looks at the door expecting someone to come through but a
moment passes and nothing happens. She resumes what she was
doing.

She unpacks a Macbook Air and activates it. As soon as the
thin laptop boots up her cell phone chimes letting her know
she has received a text.

She looks at the text from KELLY which reads: WE ARE GOOD.
CAMERAS ARE A GO. THANKS.

Juliette hides the laptop under a couch and leaves.

INT. RALEIGH'S SUITE - LATER

Juliette slides back into bed with Raleigh who is still
asleep.

As she pulls the sheets over her she looks to the ceiling and
tries to relax.

INT. THE PALAZZO - SUITE - MOMENTS LATER

Tyce holds a tablet computer on which four windows are open
showing Raleigh's office as the sun begins to rise.

The video is a bit jerky, but clear enough to see.

Tyce hands the tablet to Kelly.

                    TYCE
          I'm not sure how you did it man,
          but the cameras are in place and
          transmitting.

                    KELLY
          Let's just say we have an inside
          person.

Harrison walks into the room sipping coffee.

                    HARRISON
          This inside person wouldn't happen
          to be Raleigh's girlfriend would
          it?

                    KELLY
          Might be.

                    TYCE
          Nice play.

                    KELLY
          Thank you very much.

                    HARRISON
          This is the same woman that Frank
          was killed over right?

                    KELLY
          Your point?

                    HARRISON
          Oh nothing, just making sure I
          understood how far your depravity
          goes.

Harrison leaves the room.

Kelly looks at Tyce.

> KELLY
> I'm sure I should be offended but
> honestly I'm just too proud.

> TYCE
> No doubt.

Tyce exits and Kelly sits down next to Pete who works on his
laptop.

> KELLY
> How's it coming along?

> PETE
> It's coming. I finished the hack
> early this morning. I'll be ready
> to replace the code before lunch.

> KELLY
> Did you sleep?

> PETE
> I hack computers...sleeping is for
> pedestrians.

> KELLY
> Oooookay.

Kelly sips his coffee and the two sit in silence for a
moment.

> PETE
> So how do you do that?

> KELLY
> What?

> PETE
> How do you get girls to do what you
> want?

> KELLY
> First off, these are
> women...ladies. You have to always
> treat them like that. Second, they
> are not your enemy. They can smell
> fear and desperation, two things
> you have in excess.

                    PETE
          Have you always been able to talk
          with chicks...the ladies?

                    KELLY
          Yeah, I guess so. Ever since Frank
          taught me...

FLASHBACK -- EXT. POOLSIDE - DAY

Frank sits with a teenage Kelly. They each have a drink and
watch the plethora of lovely young ladies passing by on the
way to the pool.

                    FRANK
          The world is a wonderful place,
          son. Any of these lovely creatures
          could be yours just for the asking.

                    KELLY
          It's not that easy, dad.

                    FRANK
          Sure it is, son. This isn't rocket
          science, it's raw attraction and
          emotion, that's all. Everyone wants
          the same things in life: love,
          respect, protection, and health,
          but most of all love. We all want
          to feel loved, if only for a few
          minutes. Listen, forget all those
          fancy smancy pick-up lines you read
          about in those magazines. Who can
          remember to be that clever anyway?
          Keep it simple. Just go up, ask
          their name, give them yours. If
          there's a connection she'll let you
          know immediately?

                    KELLY
          But, what do you say next?

                    FRANK
          Anything you want, but be real.
          Woman can smell a player, they know
          when all you want is to get laid.

                    KELLY
          Which is what we really want.

                    FRANK
          Yes, but you can't be to obvious.
          Woman want to feel desired.
                    (MORE)

> FRANK (CONT'D)
> They enjoy the pursuit as much as
> we enjoy the hunt. Every person on
> this planet has something to offer
> you, all woman are attractive in
> some form or another, even if you
> don't like them physically, I
> guarantee there is something you
> will like emotionally. Treat
> everyone with respect and watch
> what happens. Let me show you.

A YOUNG LADY exits the pool and passes by their table without
even glancing their way.

Frank gets up and approaches the girl, stopping her. The two
talk (MOS) and after a brief exchange Frank follows her back
to a private cabana.

Franks looks back at his son and smiles giving him the thumbs
up.

Young Kelly returns the gesture.

BACK TO SCENE

> KELLY
> Don't make it more than it is.
> You're a good looking guy, you just
> need some opportunities to work it.

> PETE
> Can you hook me up with one of your
> friends?

> KELLY
> Let's start you out in the kiddie
> pool, not off the high dive. My
> friends would just hurt you.

Kelly gets up and exits while Pete stares at his laptop.

> PETE
> I wouldn't mind that type of pain.

INT. THE PALAZZO - SUITE - BEDROOM - CONTINUOUS

Kelly enters the bedroom where Harrison relaxes, talking on
his phone.

> HARRISON
> (into phone)
> I'll be home soon, I promise.
> (MORE)

                    HARRISON (CONT'D)
          (beat)
     No, everything's fine, things just
     are taking a bit longer than I had
     expected...And, now that I have six
     brothers, I can't just bail out as
     fast.

Kelly smiles at Harrison who shrugs and mouths, WIFE, to
Kelly.

Kelly acknowledges.

                    HARRISON (CONT'D)
     Listen, I've got to go. I'll call
     you as soon as I can. I love you.

Harrison hangs up.

                    KELLY
     Things okay at home?

                    HARRISON
     Yeah, she's just wondering when I'm
     going to be back. This was supposed
     to be a one, maybe two day trip.
     Also, things are piling up with the
     company.

                    KELLY
     If everything goes as planned you
     should be home by the weekend.

Harrison makes a face of concern and doubt.

                    KELLY (CONT'D)
     Things are coming together. I plan
     on meeting with Raleigh and the
     Russians today and then the trap
     will be set.

                    HARRISON
     And how are you going to approach
     these guys without getting killed?

                    KELLY
     I picked up some techniques on TV
     last night.

                    HARRISON
     TV?

                    KELLY
          Yeah...Burn Notice. They were
          running a marathon and I watched a
          few episodes. He gives great tips--

                    HARRISON
          You do realize that is a fictional
          show right?

                    KELLY
          But a good one. I learned a lot.

                    HARRISON
          My confidence in your plan is going
          down faster than I could have
          imagined.

INT. LUXURY CONDO - DAY

Harrison, as Thurston again, stands with Daniel in Neogod69's
condo.

                    NEOGOD69
          Did you guys really think you could
          pull a fast one over one me? You
          guys must think I'm some low rent
          code monkey instead of the
          greatest, mind bending code phreak
          on the planet.

Neogod69 flips the WiFi device in his hand as one would a
quarter.

                    NEOGOD69 (CONT'D)
          I scan this place twice a day for
          bugs and stuff like this. This is
          real amateur hour. The code your
          boy boosted -- that I allowed him
          to boost -- is nothing but a raw
          first draft. It's not worth the
          memory it takes up on his hard
          drive. Fools.

                    HARRISON
          You've made your point, but you
          have to understand the people I
          work for always cover their bases.
          If you and I couldn't come to terms
          we were going to get your code one
          way or another.

                    NEOGOD69
          Yeah but now you're not going to
          get shit.

                    HARRISON
          I do hope you will reconsider.
          These are very powerful people and
          they rarely get told no.

                    NEOGOD69
          I don't deal with thieves, liars
          and cheats.

                    HARRISON
          I guess that makes you the only
          hacker in the world with morals.

                    NEOGOD69
              (beat)
          Maybe.

                    HARRISON
          Here's the thing. I can have my man
          crack your head right now and
          simply take every hard drive in
          this place unless you are willing
          to deal.

                    NEOGOD69
          Nice try, but I don't keep my code
          here. I have a server safe and
          sound somewhere no one knows about.
          You can do your damage to me and
          take my rig, but it won't buy you
          anything.

                    HARRISON
          So you won't sell to us?

                    NEOGOD69
          I have principles.

                    HARRISON
          Then maybe we will just kill you so
          no one can have the code.

Harrison motions to Daniel who move in on Neogod69.

As Neogod69 backs up, Daniel moves in behind him so he can't
go anywhere.

                    NEOGOD69
          Okay, now hold on. This is so not
          cool.

INT. HOTEL SPA - DAY

Raleigh sits in the sauna of his hotel spa. The steam fills the room.

Geoffrey sits with him. They are the only two men in the sauna.

A female ATTENDANT enters to offer them a drink of cold water.

Both accept and Raleigh squeezes the young lady's butt.

                RALEIGH
      Why don't you sit and stay? I'll
      make it worth you while.

The girl politely declines and exits as quickly as she can.

                RALEIGH
      Get her name later and make sure
      she is fired before the end of the
      day.

Geoffrey nods his understanding and Raleigh closes his eyes and leans his head back.

The door opens again and Kelly enters. Kelly, posing as Tim Cavanagh, acts like a slick real estate agent, which of course, he once was.

                KELLY
      Mr. Raleigh Bonner? I've been
      waiting a long time to meet you.

                RALEIGH
      I'm afraid you are going to have to
      wait even longer. This is a private
      sauna.

                KELLY
      That's too bad, I have some
      important information for you that
      you're going to want to hear.

                RALEIGH
      I doubt that.

Geoffrey stands between Raleigh and Kelly.

                    KELLY
          All right, but when your little
          house of cards come crashing down
          on you, don't say no one tried to
          warn you.

Raleigh lifts his head and opens his eyes.

                    RALEIGH
          What are you talking about?

                    KELLY
          Nothing. You are a busy man, you go
          on about your busy business.

Kelly turns to leave.

Raleigh motions to Geoffrey who forcefully grabs Kelly's arm.

                    KELLY (CONT'D)
          Hey now. Don't need to get
          physical. I'm the one who came to
          you remember.

                    RALEIGH
          So talk. You have my attention...
               (looks at timer)
          ...for one minute.

Raleigh closes his eyes again as Kelly talks.

                    KELLY
          That's all I need. I keep myself in
          the know about what's what in this
          town as best I can, and--

                    RALEIGH
          Fifty seconds.

                    KELLY
               (speaking rapidly)
          Okay, once HR2267 passes Congress I
          know you are hoping to rejuvenate
          the Palace by offering a multi-
          value cash out to those who become
          members and gamble online because
          you will be the first to take
          advantage of the new law once it
          passes. I also know your code is
          nearly finished.
               (MORE)

                    KELLY (CONT'D)
What you don't know is that another
player entered the scene with more
money then you and he is closing a
deal to buy the code, your code,
right out from underneath you at
this very moment.

Raleigh looks up at Kelly. His interest piqued.

                    RALEIGH
And how do you know all this?

                    KELLY
Like I said, I keep myself in the
know. I find it helps me make new
friends...like you.

                    RALEIGH
So what do you want?

                    KELLY
Only to help...and maybe secure a
small fee.

INT. RALEIGH BONNER'S OFFICE - LATER

Kelly sits in Raleigh's office. He enjoys a drink and has
made himself comfortable.

Geoffrey stands ominously near by.

Raleigh, sitting at his desk, talks on the phone.

As the phone connects - SPLIT SCREEN WITH NEOGOD69.

                    RALEIGH
Neo? How is everything?

                    NEOGOD69
Fine. Just fine.

                    RALEIGH
Brilliant. Listen Neo, I heard some
disturbing news that someone might
be trying to outbid me on my code.

                    NEOGOD69
You got that right. The guy just
offered me twice what you did. In
cash. Guess who's going to win?

>   RALEIGH
> You can't do that! I'm the one who
> brought you the idea in the first
> place.

>   NEOGOD69
> Technically, your boy Frank did.

>   RALEIGH
> Listen to me you little pissant, if
> you try to bugger me I will come
> down on you like the four horsemen
> of the apocalypse do you understand
> me?

>   NEOGOD69
> If you want to raise your offer
> then we can talk. If not, try and
> find me.

Neogod69 hangs up.

Neogod69 looks up at Daniel who stands over him in a menacing manner.

END SPLIT SCREEN.

Raleigh slams the phone down.

Kelly raises his drink in a toast and takes another pull from it.

Juliette enters the office and reacts surprised to see Kelly there. She tries to downplay her reaction, before Raleigh notices. Too late.

>   RALEIGH
> So, Mr. Cavanagh, how do you
> propose to help me? And how much is
> it going to cost me?

>   KELLY
> The way I see it, the last thing
> you want, or can afford, is to get
> in a bidding war with this guy from
> Macau. Am I right?

>   RALEIGH
> Let's assume you are.

>   KELLY
> Okay. I am going to further assume
> you really need that code ASAP.

                    RALEIGH
          And you have a means to get me the
          code ASAP?

                    KELLY
          I do.

                    RALEIGH
          It has taken me months to find a
          programmer who could do what I
          wanted and months more for him to
          actually do it. What makes you
          think you can recreate what I need
          in less than a week?

                    KELLY
          Because I don't plan on recreating
          it.

Kelly smiles and takes another long pull from his drink.

INT. FBI HEADQUARTERS - DAY

Agent JD sits in his office. Agent Greg walks in.

                    GREG
          Have you ever heard of a guy name
          Cavanagh?

                    JD
          Nope. Should I?

                    GREG
          Don't know, but he just met with
          Raleigh and he may be a middle man
          or something.

                    JD
          Is he in the system?

                    GREG
          Nope.

                    JD
          See what you can dig up on him
          through the locals. Maybe they know
          if him.

INT. ANDRE'S - THE LOUNGE - AT THE MONTE CARLO - NIGHT

Bruce sits with LEV, the leader of the Russian mafia in Las
Vegas.

They enjoy cigars and cognac, laughing and talking (MOS).

They are the only men in the room but a number of LOVELY EASTERN EUROPEAN looking ladies sit or stand nearby.

Large BODYGUARDS block the entrance to the Lounge.

INT. ANDRE'S - THE BAR - CONTINUOUS

Daniel sits at the gold and blue bar at Andre's. In his ear is a Bluetooth headpiece. He is connected to Tyce back at the suite.

Daniel watches as Kelly ascends to the private Lounge. In his other ear is a receiver that is monitoring a microphone that Kelly wears.

> DANIEL
> Okay Tyce, Kelly is heading
> upstairs to meet the Russians. You
> have everything loaded right?

INT. THE PALAZZO - SUITE - CONTINUOUS

Tyce sits with his laptop.

> TYCE
> Yep. Good to go man.

BACK TO ANDRE'S - CONTINUOUS

Kelly enters the Lounge and is immediately stopped by SERGI, one of the bodyguards. The other bodyguards instinctively reach under their coats for their weapons in case a little hot lead is need to remedy the interruption.

> KELLY
> Whoa, hold on there my Slovakian
> friends. This here is America, the
> land of the free.

Bruce stands and approaches.

> BRUCE
> This is a private party.

> KELLY
> Great. What are we celebrating?

                    BRUCE
          You are going to be celebrating
          your life once you leave.

                    KELLY
          Sounds good. Before I go, can I
          just say, I wouldn't be caught dead
          doing business with Raleigh Bonner.

Kelly turns to leave, but before he can Bruce motions to
Sergi.

Kelly is stopped and turned around to face Bruce who has
closed the distance between them.

He speaks in hushed tones.

                    BRUCE
          Now why would you say a thing like
          that?

                    KELLY
          Just a friendly word of advice.

                    BRUCE
          Listen...friend...my friends over
          there --

Bruce motions to the Russians sitting at the table behind
him.

                    BRUCE (CONT'D)
          -- don't take kindly to strangers
          knowing their business. You got
          something to say, I suggest to you
          say it.

                    KELLY
          I think I just did. Don't do
          business with Raleigh Bonner.

                    BRUCE
          And why should I listen to you?

                    KELLY
          My name's Hargrave.

Bruce motions for one of the bodyguards to check Kelly out.

The bodyguard takes out an iPad and begins doing a web
search.

BACK TO BAR AT ANDRE'S - CONTINUOUS

>DANIEL
>It sounds like they're doing the
>search now. We set?

BACK TO SUITE - CONTINUOUS

>TYCE
>I told you man...wait a minute--

BACK TO BAR AT ANDRE'S - CONTINUOUS

>DANIEL
>What?

BACK TO SUITE - CONTINUOUS

Tyce types frantically on his laptop.

Pete enters munching on a bag of Cheetos and drinking a
Mountain Dew.

>TYCE
>Did you change the Hargrave cover?

>PETE
>Yeah, I was enhancing it a bit. I
>thought your story had too many
>holes.

>TYCE
>And have you posted it yet?

>PETE
>No, I got the munchies.

BACK TO BAR AT ANDRE'S - CONTINUOUS

Daniel begins to get a bit worried.

>DANIEL
>Guys?

BACK TO SUITE - CONTINUOUS

>TYCE
>You moron! Kelly is in the lion's
>den as we speak.
>(MORE)

                    TYCE (CONT'D)
          They are doing the search right
          now. He's a deadman if we don't get
          that posted!

BACK TO LOUNGE AT ANDRE'S - CONTINUOUS

Bruce looks at the bodyguard with the iPad who is still
searching.

The bodyguard looks up at one point and shakes his head
negatively.

Bruce looks at Kelly who simply smiles as innocently as he
can.

                    KELLY
          Listen guys, I won't bother you
          anymore I can see you're busy.

Sergi stops Kelly from leaving.

                    BRUCE
          No so fast...friend.

BACK TO SUITE - CONTINUOUS

Tyce and Pete type as fast as they can.

                    TYCE
          You are so dead if Kelly ends up
          dead.

Pete ignores Tyce and keeps typing.

BACK TO BAR AT ANDRE'S - CONTINUOUS

                    DANIEL
          Nobody needs to end up dead if you
          just get things working.

BACK TO LOUNGE AT ANDRE'S - CONTINUOUS

Bruce still waits for some confirmation from the bodyguard
with the iPad, who finally looks up and nods approval.

He brings the iPad over for Bruce to read.

                    BRUCE
          Interesting. You keep yourself
          quite busy around town Mr.
          Hargrave. I'm surprised I haven't
          heard of you before.

BACK TO SUITE - CONTINUOUS

Tyce and Pete lay back into the couch, relaxing.

                    TYCE
          That was close.

BACK TO BAR AT ANDRE'S - CONTINUOUS

                    DANIEL
          A little too close.

BACK TO LOUNGE AT ANDRE'S - CONTINUOUS

                    KELLY
          Well, I hate to brag, but I do
          pride myself in staying in the loop
          on things. I also hate the
          spotlight.

                    BRUCE
          As do we.

                    KELLY
          You aren't going to be able to do
          that with Raleigh Bonner.

                    BRUCE
          What's you issue with Bonner?

                    KELLY
          I've had my dealings with him.
          Never once ended the way they were
          supposed to. He's is a double
          dealing, back stabbing, killer. Not
          the type of guy with a lot of
          friends. I'm willing to bet he came
          to you for a loan.

                    BRUCE
          You sure know a lot about our
          business.

                              KELLY
                    Not yours, Raleigh's, but trust me,
                    Raleigh's business is everyone's
                    business. The only thing bigger
                    than that arrogant bastard's mouth
                    is his credit risk. He's always
                    talking about his deals and
                    successes. Makes him feel like a
                    big shot. Listen, Raleigh's British
                    accent and pompous attitude have
                    gotten him nowhere except an aging
                    casino with a huge debt load.

Bruce thinks about all that Kelly has told him.

                              BRUCE
                    You paint a pretty convincing
                    picture. It has been nice meeting
                    you Mr. Hargrave.

Bruce motions for Sergi to show Kelly out.

As he turns away, Kelly says over his shoulder.

                              KELLY
                    Oh, and don't let Raleigh con you
                    into believing he has some super
                    code that is going to work. He
                    doesn't.

                              BRUCE
                    Wait.

Bruce, exasperated now, motions for Sergi to bring Kelly back
in.

                              KELLY
                    Oh, sorry did I fail to mention
                    that the software Raleigh is
                    touting as the Viagra for casinos
                    is buggy as hell and won't be ready
                    in time for his tournament. Guess
                    Raleigh failed to mention that as
                    well.

                              BRUCE
                    What do you know about this?

                              KELLY
                    I know that some big fish from
                    Macau with Chinese backing came to
                    town and bought the program right
                    out from under Raleigh. The Brits
                    got nothing.
                              (MORE)

                    KELLY (CONT'D)
          (beat)
     Except your money, I would guess.

INT. FBI HEADQUARTERS - SAME TIME

Agents JD and Greg sit in the dimly lit surveillance room
listening to the voices of Bruce and Kelly.

                    JD
          Okay, Bruce I know. Raleigh I know.
          Who the hell is this Mr. Hargrave?

                    GREG
          I don't know. Wait a minute.

Agent Greg sorts through some photos until he finds the one
he remembers.

                    GREG
          Hargrave is also Cavanagh.

                    JD
          Who?

                    GREG
          They guy I told you met with
          Raleigh.

                    JD
          Now he's meeting with the Russians?
          Sounds like he is a middle man. Did
          we learn anything about him?

                    GREG
          No. Could be because he has
          multiple aliases.

                    JD
          I hate unknown variables. What's
          this code he's talking about?

                    GREG
          I don't know that yet either.

                    JD
          So basically we don't have a
          freaking clue about anything right
          now.

Long pause.

                    GREG
          At this time, no. I think we should
          pick up this Hargrave, or Cavanagh,
          and bring him in.

                    JD
          That's about all we can do at this
          point.

                    GREG
          I think things just got a lot more
          complicated.

INT. THE PALAZZO - SUITE - NIGHT

Tyce enters data on his laptop for Harrison's, Thurston cover
identity.

On a tablet sitting near him he monitors Raleigh's office.
Raleigh is busy at his desk.

Pete, bored, sticks his finger into Tyce's ear.

Tyce reacts only by saying --

                    TYCE
          Don't.

                    PETE
          Don't what?

                    TYCE
          Don't do that.

                    PETE
          Don't do what?

                    TYCE
          Don't do that thing you just did.

Pete sticks his finger in Tyce's ear again.

                    PETE
          You mean this?

                    TYCE
          Yes.

                    PETE
          So that's what you don't want me to
          do?

                    TYCE
          Right. Don't do that again.

                    PETE
          Okay. I won't.

Pete waits a few seconds and then does it again.

This time Tyce swats at his hand.

                    TYCE
          Man, what's your problem?

                    PETE
          You didn't say how long you didn't
          want me to do that.

                    TYCE
          Man, you can enter this information
          yourself then. You'd better upload
          it correctly this time. No more
          last minute crap, you hear me?

Tyce gets up and leaves.

Pete parrots what Tyce said under his breath in a child-like
manner.

Tyce hears him and comes back to smack Pete in the back of
the head before finally exiting.

                    TYCE (CONT'D)
          And you'd better let Kelly know if
          Raleigh leaves.

INT. SENSEI AT THE BELLAGIO - NIGHT

Juliette sits at a table by herself near the back corner of
the restaurant with her back to the carved stoned walls.

Kelly enters and approaches her table.

                    KELLY
          May I?

                    JULIETTE
          I've been waiting.

                    KELLY
          Sorry. I had to stop and see
          someone.

                    JULIETTE
          A lady friend?

                    KELLY
          Jealous?

                    JULIETTE
          Hardly.

                    KELLY
          So how's our little British friend?

                    JULIETTE
          Don't underestimate him Kelly.
          Raleigh is a dangerous man.

                    KELLY
          You don't need to remind me --

                    JULIETTE
          Sorry. Are you sure you want to do
          this? You guys are messing with
          some powerful people. Raleigh had
          drinks with a Senator after he met
          with you.

                    KELLY
          About?

                    JULIETTE
          The bill to legalize online
          gambling in the US. His "campaign
          contributions" will all but
          guarantee the bill passes this
          session. Raleigh is no third rate
          criminal, Kelly. You and your
          brothers are getting in deep.

                    KELLY
          I...we, can't let our father die in
          vain.
               (beat)
          Anyway, I'm having fun.

                    JULIETTE
          You're crazy. You know that right?

                    KELLY
          I had heard rumors.

          The waiter walks by.

                    KELLY (CONT'D)
          You ready? I am starving.

-- LATER

The restaurant is nearly empty now.

An empty wine bottle on the table and nearly empty glasses before both Kelly and Juliette.

They laugh and are having a good time.

> KELLY
> So listen, when this thing is finished...

> JULIETTE
> Don't.

> KELLY
> What?

> JULIETTE
> Don't talk to me about the future. Don't make promises you won't keep, and don't act like this is more than what it is.

> KELLY
> And what do you think it is?

> JULIETTE
> I know what it is, and I'm fine with it, but don't try to con me too.

> KELLY
> I wasn't --

> JULIETTE
> Listen Kelly. I'm more than happy to help you take down Raleigh. Heaven knows he deserves, but this isn't my first rodeo. I know the score. I'm simply a pawn in the middle. Let's keep the focus and get the job done.

> KELLY
> All right.

> JULIETTE
> Good. Thanks for dinner. I'd better get back.

Juliette stands to leave.

                    JULIETTE
          By the way, your brother Harrison --

                    KELLY
          Yeah?

                    JULIETTE
          He's quite good at what he does. I
          made sure we had space for him. He
          has the town buzzing with the party
          he's going to throw in conjunction
          with the tournament. He certainly
          got Raleigh's attention.

                    KELLY
          That's the plan.

                    JULIETTE
          Be careful.

Juliette leaves.

Kelly watches her go then drinks the rest of his wine in one
gulp.

The waiter comes by and drops off the bill.

Kelly looks at the bill and grimaces.

EXT. BELLAGIO - NIGHT

Kelly exits the hotel and approaches the valet when a dark
sedan pulls up and a group of AGENTS approach him.

                    KELLY
                  (nonchalantly)
          Hello. I don't think we've been
          properly introduced.

The agents say nothing but escort him to the back of their
car.

INT. FBI INTERROGATION ROOM - LATER

Kelly sits at a bare metal table in a bare nondescript room
which warrants no further description.

Agent Greg enters the room with a file which he drops on the
table as he walks around behind Kelly.

                    GREG
          Well, we did some checking...

                    KELLY
          That's what you guys do.

                    GREG
          Yep, and guess what I found? You're
          real name is Kelly Wolffe --

                    KELLY
          It is? Thank you. I have been
          wandering aimlessly --

                    GREG
          Save it. You just did a nickel for
          real estate fraud. Haven't even
          been out a week and already I have
          you consorting with Russian
          mobsters. I bet I can find out more
          if I really start checking into
          things, but I think that alone
          would revoke your parole.

                    KELLY
          You must have me mistaken for
          someone else.

                    GREG
          You think so?

Greg opens the folder and pulls out a photo of Kelly in the
grips of the Russian bodyguard coming out of the Lounge at
Andre's.

                    GREG (CONT'D)
          That's Sergi. Doesn't know much
          English, but most people understand
          him just fine.

                    KELLY
          That's not consorting, that's being
          assaulted. I'm glad you have that
          as evidence. I want to press
          charges.

                    GREG
          Do you want to hear the audio of
          your conversation with Bruce
          Durgan?

                    KELLY
          That won't be necessary. I can see
          you are quite good at your
          checking.

                         GREG
              Yes we are. So now we can talk
              straight with each other right?

                         KELLY
              Sure.

EXT. FBI HEADQUARTERS - NIGHT

Kelly is seen leaving the FBI headquarters. Someone watches
him and takes pictures.

Kelly leaves the building and walks away.

INT. THE PALAZZO - SUITE - DAY

Harrison paces the living room talking on the phone.

Pete types on his laptop and Tyce watches the security
monitors.

                         HARRISON
                    (to person on phone)
              Great! So we can count on you to
              attend?
                    (beat while he listens)
              Awesome! And your sisters will
              attend as well?
                    (beat)
              I appreciate it. I will see you
              then.

Harrison hangs up the phone.

                         HARRISON (CONT'D)
              That should do it.

                         TYCE
              Who was that?

                         HARRISON
              Kim.

Tyce looks up from his computer with a shocked and excited
look on his face.

                         TYCE
              As in Kardashian?

                         HARRISON
              Yep.

                    TYCE
You just hung up the phone with Kim
Kardashian?

                    HARRISON
She and her sisters plan on
attending our party.

                    TYCE
Aw man, you have to introduce me.

                    HARRISON
Yeah, about that...

                    TYCE
C'mon man.

                    HARRISON
We'll see. With them, the Hilton's,
the cast of Entourage and throw in
a few NFL superstars and I'd say we
have the makings of a pretty cool
party.

                    PETE
You think?

                    DANIEL
Which NFL stars?

                    TYCE
Dude, really? The Kardashians? And
all you can ask about is a NFL
player?

                    HARRISON
Listen guys, stay focused. This
party is meant to be a distraction
to Raleigh, not us.

                    DANIEL
Yea, I don't see what the big deal
is. They're just people, and Kim is
just another high maintenance chick
you couldn't afford her, Ty.

                    HARRISON
I've got to go. Daniel, know when
and where to meet us right?

                    DANIEL
You bet. See ya then.

INT. THE PALACE CASINO - DAY

Raleigh walks with Harrison through the casino. Juliette and
Geoffrey in tow.

                    RALEIGH
          So you see, Mr. Patterson, the
          renovations will be completed in
          time for your event and the
          tournament.

                    HARRISON
          I hope so. Celebrities don't like
          dust.

                    RALEIGH
          Yes, celebrities can be so charming
          in their own way.

                    HARRISON
          You sure have a lot riding on this
          Mr. Bonner.

                    RALEIGH
          Quite.

                    HARRISON
          I hope it all goes smoothly for
          you.

                    JULIETTE
          I can assure you Mr. Patterson, we
          are doing everything and will do
          everything to make sure your event
          has no problems.

                    HARRISON
          I'd expect nothing less.

                    RALEIGH
          Brilliant. Well, if there is
          nothing else, I do have a number of
          other matters to attend to.

                    HARRISON
          That does it for me.

The two men shake hands.

                    HARRISON (CONT'D)
          I appreciate your personal
          attention to this Mr. Bonner.

                    RALEIGH
          Your party is a welcome event on
          what I expect to be a momentous
          occasion for the Palace.

                    HARRISON
          Glad you see the importance of what
          I am bringing to you. From what
          I've heard The Palace could sure
          use a shot in the arm. My party
          just might be what you need to
          bring this place back to life.

Raleigh, <u>obviously offended</u> by the remarks, keeps his cool.

                    RALEIGH
          Well, you honor us with your
          business.
               (beat, looking at watch)
          Now if you will excuse me, I really
          should be going.

                    HARRISON
          Certainly. I will be in touch.

Harrison smiles and leaves.

Once he is out of hearing range...

                    RALEIGH
          That arrogant little prick.

                    JULIETTE
          He may be brash, but he is bringing
          in a lot of name people. I thought
          you would be happy for the added
          publicity his party will bring.

                    RALEIGH
          I love the publicity, I just don't
          need some Hollywood poofter
          distracting me right now with all
          his demands. I should just have you
          deal with it.

                    JULIETTE
          I will if you want me to.

                    RALEIGH
          Yeah, do.

Raleigh looks at his watch.

                    RALEIGH
          Crap. I am supposed to meet
          Congressman Stamp.

                    JULIETTE
          What's the problem?

                    RALEIGH
          I don't have his "campaign
          contribution" ready yet.
               (to Geoffrey)
          Go down to the vault and pick up
          the usual contribution fund, then
          meet me at the Courtyard Bar. You
          think you can handle that?

Geoffrey nods.

                    RALEIGH
          Brilliant.

INT. THE VENETIAN - GRAND CANAL SHOPPES - ST. MARK'S SQUARE-
DAY

Bruce sits on a bench sipping a drink and watching the
tourist wander past. He looks like he has no worries in the
world. Behind him stands Sergi -- the reason why Bruce looks
like he has no worries in the world.

Kelly, Harrison, Daniel approach.

Daniel stays back a few paces and eyes Sergi while Kelly and
Harrison continue to the bench to meet Bruce.

A few people in the crowd, appear to be federal agents
keeping surveillance on Bruce.

                    BRUCE
          So this is the monkey wrench in
          Raleigh's grand scheme.

                    KELLY
          This is the guy I was telling you
          about.

                    BRUCE
          I had my people check into you.

                    HARRISON
          I hope you found what you are
          looking for.

                    BRUCE
Actually, there isn't much to find
on you--

                    HARRISON
Same could be said about you I
imagine.

                    BRUCE
True.

                    HARRISON
What I do for my clients is make
them money. Sometimes the way I do
it isn't so legal. They appreciate
it when I don't make headlines.
Bottom line, I could care less
about Raleigh Bonner. What I am
interested in is that program.

                    BRUCE
And what makes this program so
popular right now?

                    HARRISON
A program like this offers casino
operators a way to tie online
gambling with a real casino through
a Multi-value cash out.

                    BRUCE
Meaning...?

                    HARRISON
Meaning, we can increase gambling
revenue without having to drive
traffic to our physical casinos,
but there is a value, a reward
points system if you will, where
players who do come to the casinos
can exchange points for room
nights, food, spa treatments and
other amenities. A program that can
track and control all of this has
the potential of increasing revenue
by billions.

                    BRUCE
So, why should I do business with
you instead of Raleigh?

                    KELLY
As we discussed before, Raleigh is
a bloated beached whale.
                    (MORE)

                    KELLY (CONT'D)
He has more debt than brains.
Whereas Mr. Thurston here has a
growing business in the East that
can be expanded here in the States.

                    BRUCE
How?

                    KELLY
Easy. If Raleigh doesn't get hold
of this code his poker tournament
will be just another in a long line
of uneventful events that happen in
casinos all over the nation. He's
banking on having the code, and
announcing the tie in with online
gaming. When he can't make that
connection, he's going to default
on his loan with the bank and with
you, and essentially lose his
hotel. Between the two of you, you
can buy the code and his hotel and
run the entire thing yourselves.

                    BRUCE
You make it sound so simple.

                    KELLY
It's a skill I have.

                    BRUCE
So why do you need us?

                    HARRISON
Raleigh is counting on your help to
secure the code. If you drop out
suddenly he'll panic and go
somewhere else to raise the money.
If he thinks you're still with him
then we know what he's doing and we
control his every move.

                    KELLY
So we need you to give Raleigh the
money, but we're going to sell him
bogus code.

                    BRUCE
And where is the real code?

                    KELLY
We have it. We can show you the
code and then buy it.

                    BRUCE
          Wait. It sounds like I am paying
          twice.

                    KELLY
          You are, but we will have control
          of Raleigh's money, so we can just
          turn around and return it to you
          once Raleigh has been played.

                    BRUCE
          You had better make sure Raleigh is
          the only one being played.

INT. FBI HEADQUARTERS - DAY

Agents Greg and JD stand in front of the white board with the
photos of Bruce, the Russians, Raleigh and now Kelly,
Harrison, Daniel, Pete, and Tyce.

                    JD
          Now who the hell are these jokers?
          Have you checked all of Kelly's
          known friends?

                    GREG
          Yes, and we are continuing to look
          into it.

                    JD
          I'm beginning to think Kelly's
          story is as bogus as the property
          he used to sell.

                    GREG
          You want us to pick him up again?

                    JD
          Not yet. Let's let this play out a
          bit and see what he is really up
          to. In the meantime, let's find out
          who these others are.

                    GREG
          Will do.

                    JD
          This is getting more confusing by
          the hour. If any more players enter
          this game I may take up drinking
          again.

EXT. SIDEWALK IN FRONT OF THE BELLAGIO FOUNTAINS - DAY

The five brothers stand and admire the fountains as it performs its show.

                    HARRISON
          I think we may just pull this off.

                    KELLY
          Was there ever any doubt?

Harrison looks at Kelly with a sidelong look.

                    KELLY (CONT'D)
          Is everything in place for the next
          phase?

                    PETE
          Both sets of code are ready.

                    TYCE
          Ready.

Daniel nods.

                    KELLY
          Good. Let's roll.

EXT. LOOKING TOWARDS THE BELLAGIO FOUNTAINS - DAY

From across the street, someone watches the brothers and takes photographs while they talk.

INT. RALEIGH BONNER'S OFFICE -- NIGHT

Kelly sits in Raleigh's office with a drink in his hand. He seems relaxed, while Raleigh seems on edge.

                    KELLY
          Raleigh, relax. You are going to
          stroke on me and then where will we
          be?

                    RALEIGH
          If this goes balls up, I am in real
          trouble.

                    KELLY
          It's not going to. I hired a great
          team to do the job and they agreed
          to sell us the code for the
          original price. Now sit back and
          watch the show.

Raleigh pours himself another tall drink of Scotch and tosses
it back.

He hits the remote control and one of the large flat panel
televisions shows a jerky, grainy greenish image.

                    RALEIGH
          Is that it?

                    KELLY
          Should be. The team is just getting
          into place.

On the screen a team of two men -- Daniel and Tyce-- wearing
black jumpsuits, tactical gear and facemasks with night
vision goggles prepare to enter Neogod69's condo.

One of the two wears a camera that broadcasts the raid along
with audio.

The two enter the condo where they confront Neogod69.

He is scared and yells for help.

One of the masked men tackle him and gag him before he can
escape.

The other grabs the computer hard drives and smash the
monitors.

                    KELLY
          I feel so James Bond right now. Oh
          wait, better yet, Jason Bourne.

Raleigh simply stares at Kelly like he is some kind of freak.

He returns his attention to the monitor where one of the
masked men speaks into the camera that the other is wearing.

                    DANIEL / MASKED INTRUDER
          Package is secure. We shall
          rendezvous at the designated spot
          in an hour.

The scene goes black as the camera stops transmitting.

Raleigh turns off the television.

                    KELLY
          Well, Raleigh old boy, it looks
          like you have yourself some super
          code.

                    RALEIGH
          Cheers that.

                    KELLY
          You have the money right?

                    RALEIGH
          Yes, it was delivered earlier
          today.

                    KELLY
          Okay, give it to me and I will go
          make the pick up.

                    RALEIGH
          Sod that. I want to be there.

                    KELLY
          Raleigh, do you really want to be
          directly connected to a breaking
          and entering. No, I don't think so.
          Let me do the bag work and you wait
          here. I won't be more than a couple
          of hours.

                    RALEIGH
          Take Geoffrey then.

Kelly hesitates at the complication, but then agrees.

                    KELLY
          Sure. No problem.

INT. LUXURY CONDO - NIGHT

Back at Neogod69's condo, Daniel cleans up the place.

                    NEOGOD69
          Dudes did you really have to smash
          my monitor? That was a 26 inch
          Syncmaster.

                    DANIEL
          We had to make it look convincing.

                    NEOGOD69
          Yeah but...

>   DANIEL
>   Don't worry about it. With what
>   you're getting paid, you can buy
>   all you want.
>   (beat)
>   Now help us clean up so we are
>   ready for our next guests.

INT. LUXURY CONDO HALLWAY - LATER

Harrison stands with Bruce and Sergi at the door.

Harrison knocks.

When the door opens it is Daniel who answers.

>   HARRISON
>   We're here for the package.

>   DANIEL
>   It's ready.

INSIDE CONDO - CONTINUOUS

The room has been put back together as if the raid never took
place. New monitors have replaced the smashed ones and code
streams across the screens.

Pete sits at Neogod69's workstation taping away at the
computer keys with his back to Harrison and Bruce.

Harrison enters with Bruce and Muscle.

>   BRUCE
>   Can we make this quick? I have
>   tickets for Love tonight.

>   HARRISON
>   Sure.
>   (to Pete)
>   Show us the demo.

Pete nods under his hoody and his hands flash over the
keyboard in a magical coder dance. The screens change from
raw code to a graphic user interface of a online gaming site.

On another monitor is a web-site for a hotel.

                         PETE
          If you watch the screen where the
          online gaming is taking place you
          will notice my winnings translate
          in real time to reward points on
          the hotel and casino site. Each
          hand I play adds a few more points
          to my account. The more hands I
          play, the more reward points. Then
          when I finally cash out, my
          winnings are totaled and that can
          increase my reward points as well.
          The player has the option to cash
          out for money, or exchange for
          points. Obviously the more we get
          them to play, with the carrot of
          reward points, the more likely the
          house will win. Either way it is
          win win, just more win for us.

                         BRUCE
          Nice. And the system is ready to
          launch.

                         PETE
          Without a doubt.

Bruce shakes Harrison's hand.

                         BRUCE
          I think we have ourselves a
          partnership.

Bruce motions for Sergi to hand Harrison a briefcase.

                         BRUCE (CONT'D)
          You can count it if you like.

                         HARRISON
          I don't think that will be
          necessary

                         BRUCE
          Me neither. We'll be in touch.

Bruce and Sergi leave and Daniel closes the door.

INT. BRUCE DURGGAN'S OFFICE - LATER

Bruce returns to his office.

Lev is waiting for him. He does not look happy.

                    BRUCE
          Lev. Did we have a meeting I
          forgot?

                    LEV
          Sit down Bruce. We have to talk.

Bruce is a bit nervous.

                    BRUCE
          This sounds ominous. What's up?

                    LEV
          You loaned our money to Raleigh
          Bonner, yes?

                    BRUCE
          Yes, as we discussed. I thought we
          were all on the same page about
          this?

                    LEV
          Yes, we were. We were. And you also
          did the deal with that man Hargrave
          and his associate?

                    BRUCE
          Yes. As agreed.

                    LEV
          Of course.

                    BRUCE
          Lev, you've got me on pins and
          needles here, what's going on?

                    LEV
          Some new information has come to my
          attention.

                    BRUCE
          Well, do tell. I am wet with
          anticipation.

                    LEV
          Bruce, we have trusted you to
          protect our money --

                    BRUCE
          -- And I have. How many years have
          I worked for you Lev? Have I once
          steered you wrong? No.

                         LEV
          But, maybe today is that day? Maybe
          you have grown sloppy.

                         BRUCE
          Really? When have you known me to
          be sloppy?

                         LEV
          We are worried Bruce. You have
          given a substantial amount of cash
          to someone that, as it so happens,
          was not who they said they were. We
          want to make sure our money gets
          back to us.

                         BRUCE
          Help me here, who are we talking
          about?

Lev tosses a manila folder of color photos onto Bruce's desk.
Some of the photos spill across his desk.

They are images of Kelly coming out of the FBI headquarters
and all of the brothers standing at the fountain in front of
the Bellagio.

Bruce picks up the photos and flips through them.

                         BRUCE
          This doesn't look good.

                         LEV
          Nyet. It does not. What do you make
          of this?

                         BRUCE
          To be honest Lev, I don't know, but
          I bet we can find out real easily.

                         LEV
          Good.

                         BRUCE
          Let me look into this and get back
          to you.

                         LEV
          I shall wait for word.

INT. RALEIGH BONNER'S OFFICE - DAY

Raleigh stands behind his desk and is jittery with nervous energy.

Juliette enters the office wearing a designer outfit.

> JULIETTE
> Relax Raleigh. Everything is going
> to be fine.

> RALEIGH
> Sure, sure. It just seems like
> there are always a million tiny
> details to keep after.

> JULIETTE
> Yes, but that's why you pay a
> million tiny dollars to people to
> look after them for you.

> RALEIGH
> You're right.

> JULIETTE
> Of course I am. You should relax
> and enjoy this. It's your big day.

Raleigh gathers some note cards from his desk and shuffles through them making sure they are in order and all there.

> RALEIGH
> All set.

> JULIETTE
> Then let's go make news.

Raleigh walks around his desk and Juliette takes his arm.

Geoffrey waits for them at the elevator to take them down to the casino floor.

INT. THE PALACE CASINO - CONTINUOUS

It is finally the day to announce the Internet and poker tournament hosted by the Palace.

A temporary wall with the logo of The Palace and ePalacePoker.com dotted across it in an alternating pattern has been erected in front of an expansive card table room on the floor of the casino.

On either side of the wall, two large flat panel monitors are mounted on tall stands. A 3D logo for the hotel rotates and with each spin it morphs into the logo of the online gaming site, then back again.

Behind the wall in the card room, poker players sit at the various tables playing in the tournament.

In front of the wall, a few news cameras and microphones have been set up.

Other television cameras dot the card room floor as the entire proceedings are televised on in-room and national cable broadcast.

The brothers have gathered to watch the proceedings from a distance.

Tyce has his tablet with him and continues to monitor the cameras placed in Raleigh's office.

                    TYCE
               (to Kelly)
          Our man's on the move.

                    KELLY
          That means the show is about to get
          started. Well guys, this is it. If
          all goes as planned, Raleigh should
          have a nice surprise for him and it
          will spell the beginning of the
          end.

                    PETE
          All this excitement is making me
          want to pee.

                    TYCE
          Didn't you go just like ten minutes
          ago?

                    PETE
          I have an excitable bladder.

                    TYCE
          Bro, you're a freak in so many
          ways.

                    PETE
          I'll be right back.

Pete exits to look for a bathroom.

Daniel nudges Kelly to turn around and motions in the
direction where Raleigh is approaching.

Kelly leaves the group to approach Raleigh.

> KELLY
> It's your big day old chap.

Raleigh is surprised to see Kelly but shakes his hand anyway.

Juliette tries to act nonchalant.

> RALEIGH
> Mr. Cavanagh. I can honestly say I
> didn't expect to see you here
> today.

> KELLY
> I wouldn't have missed this for the
> world.

> RALEIGH
> Right. Well if you will excuse me I
> do have some business to attend.

> KELLY
> Absolutely. I don't want to hold
> you up, just thought I would say
> hello and I hope you get everything
> you deserve.

Raleigh looks at him a little questioningly.

> KELLY (CONT'D)
> I just mean, you've worked so
> hard...

> RALEIGH
> Brilliant. Cheers. Feel free to
> stay and play some tables if you
> like.

> KELLY
> Thanks. I may just do that.

Raleigh leaves to stand in front of the microphones.

Juliette stays behind and whispers to Kelly.

> JULIETTE
> You sure like to play things fast
> and loose don't you?

                              KELLY
                    Is there any other way?

                              JULIETTE
                    You're just like your dad.

Juliette leaves to be closer to Raleigh.

                              KELLY
                         (to self)
                    She says that like it's a bad
                    thing.

As Kelly walks back to regroup with his brothers he bumps
into Steve Wynn.

                              KELLY
                    Mr. Wynn. A great pleasure to meet
                    you.

                              STEVE WYNN
                    Thank you. I would say the same
                    but...

                              KELLY
                    Kelly Wolffe. I have always admired
                    your work.

                              STEVE WYNN
                    Thanks again. I guess now we have
                    to admire Raleigh's work. He beat
                    me to the punch on this one.

                              KELLY
                    As they say Steve, don't count your
                    chips until the hand is over.

TO PRESS ANOUNCEMENT - CONTINUOUS

Raleigh, stands in front of the press wall and clears his
throat.

                              RALEIGH
                    Today, The Palace in partnership
                    with ePalacePoker.com, unveils its
                    latest renovation, not only with
                    its rooms and new restaurants but a
                    renovation of how gambling will be
                    accomplished in the future.
                              (MORE)

                    RALEIGH (CONT'D)
          Here at The Palace we have
          developed a method that allows
          players the combination of the
          energy and excitement of game room
          casino gambling with the privacy
          and easy access of 24 hour online
          gaming. To launch this new site we
          are proud to be hosting the World
          of Poker tournament, which had its
          qualifying rounds online and is now
          taking place in the room behind us.

ON BROTHERS - CONTINUOUS

Kelly returns to where the brothers stand. They want to see
but not be seen.

                    DANIEL
          Has anyone seen Pete? He's going to
          miss everything.

                    HARRISON
          He must still be in the bathroom.

                    TYCE
          For a little guy he sure has a big
          bladder. His problem is he just
          can't hold it.

                    KELLY
          I can't believe he would miss the
          unveiling of his program. This has
          got to be a hackers biggest day.

ON RALEIGH - CONTINUOUS

                    RALEIGH
          And so it is with great excitement
          that I announce the launch of the
          first combination online and casino
          gambling.

Raleigh turns to the monitors and presses a button on a
remote control to change the presentation.

There is a pause. Nothing happens.

Suddenly the screens go black and then the video of Frank's
video Will pops on.

> FRANK
> Raleigh owns The Palace, a mid-size
> hotel/casino on the south end of
> the Strip. He desperately dreams of
> being in the big league with the
> like of Wynn, Adelson, and Trump. I
> was helping him with a killer new
> concept where we tied on-line
> gambling with a physical casino.

There is a sharp edit in the footage.

> FRANK (CONT'D)
> If I'm dead, that means he stole my
> idea and wanted to cut me out,
> keeping it all for himself.

The screen goes black and there is hushed mumbling through
the crowd.

Raleigh is noticeably shaken by the turn of events and looks
around for someone to assist him.

Finally the screen flashes again as code streams across the
screen then stops as the words SYSTEM ERROR, repeated over
and over, filling the screen only to be replaced by the words
INITIATE SYSTEM REFORMAT.

With that, the power in the entire casino blinks out for a
moment.

The lights go out.

The slot machines stop working.

People start shouting.

ON BROTHERS - CONTINUOUS

> HARRISON
> We should really get out of here.

> KELLY
> I'm loving watching Raleigh squirm.

> TYCE
> I can't believe Pete didn't make it
> back.

> DANIEL
> I'm going to look for him.

                    HARRISON
          When you find him, meet us at the
          suite. We clear out tonight.

Daniel takes off.

Tyce and Harrison turn to leave.

Harrison has to pull on Kelly.

                    HARRISON
          Come on.

ON RALEIGH - CONTINUOUS

Raleigh is furious.

His staff has come to help as he storms off without saying a
word, even though the media is shouting questions.

INT. THE PALACE COMPUTER SERVER ROOM - LATER

Raleigh stands amongst dozens of computer servers in racks
making corridors and paths.

One of his IT TECHNICIANS tries to explain what has happened.

                    RALEIGH
          Bullocks! How long is this going to
          take?!

                    IT EMPLOYEE
          I can only guess at this point.
          That program had a Trojan horse in
          it that started reformatting
          everything. We nearly lost the
          entire system.

                    RALEIGH
          I'm losing millions for every
          second its not working. How long?

                    IT EMPLOYEE
          A few hours at least. Maybe more. I
          have to install the backup.

                    RALEIGH
          Bloody hell. This will ruin me.

INT. THE PALAZZO - SUITE - LATER

Kelly, Harrison and Tyce are in the main room of the suite.
They pack things as quickly as they can.

Daniel enters the room.

                    HARRISON
          Did you find Pete?

                    DANIEL
          You mean he's not with you guys?

                    HARRISON
          No.

                    DANIEL
          I checked every bathroom in the
          place. That place was a mad house
          with the power problems.

                    KELLY
          Are you sure you didn't miss him.

                    DANIEL
          I waited for people to clear out.
          It's a ghost town now.

                    KELLY
          Raleigh must be pissing himself.

                    HARRISON
          What about Pete?

                    KELLY
          I'm sure he will turn up. Kid can
          take care of himself.

INT. STORAGE ROOM - NIGHT

Pete sits with a hood over his head in a storage room of some
building. LOUD MUSIC can be heard from another room.

Standing behind Pete is Sergi.

Bruce enters the room and motions for Sergi to remove the
hood.

Pete is scared pissless, which is clear by the stain on the
front of his pants.

                    BRUCE
          Hello Neo. It is Neo right?

                    PETE
          Yeah. Neo.

                    BRUCE
          So how's our code?

                    PETE
          Fine. Hey listen, I gave your
          friends the program.

                    BRUCE
          Did you? Let me ask you, did you
          know any of those guys before we
          approached you to buy the code?

                    PETE
          No.

                    BRUCE
          You sure?

                    PETE
          Yeah. What's going on?

                    BRUCE
          Well listen...Neo. My business
          partners seem to think you do know
          those other guys.

Bruce shows Pete the photo of all the brothers standing in
front of the fountain.

                    BRUCE (CONT'D)
          So here's the deal. My friend Sergi
          here is going to talk with you
          about this photo and your friends.
          Thing is, Sergi doesn't speak any
          English so he is going to have to
          communicate in another way.

Bruce looks at Sergi who slams his fist into the palm of his
hand.

Pete looks at Sergi then faints.

-- FLASHBACK EXT. SCHOOL YARD - DAY

A very young Pete stands in front Frank. A black eye, cut lip
and torn shirt are evidence that Pete was just roughed up by
bullies.

Frank dusts off his son and tries to calm his crying.

                        FRANK
              It's okay son. You just got the
              wind knocked out of you, you'll be
              okay.
                    (beat)
              You know, don't be deceived son,
              there's a lot you can learn from
              losing a fight. Nothing builds
              character better than getting your
              ass kicked and still walking away
              from it...

INT. HOTEL SUITE - NIGHT

Kelly packs clothes when his cell phone buzzes. He has
received a text message and photo of Pete bound and gagged.
The text reads: "WE HAVE YOUR BROTHER. WANT TO SEE HIM ALIVE?
NEED TO MEET."

                        KELLY
              Oh crap!

Kelly walks into the main room where the others are busy
packing.

                        KELLY (CONT'D)
              We have a serious problem.

Kelly hands him the phone.

INT. RALEIGH BONNER'S OFFICE - DAY

Raleigh on the phone, listens to the person on the other
line. At first he looks confused, then concerned, then angry.
Whatever is said obviously has a negative effect on Raleigh's
mood which is already way past bad.

                        RALEIGH
              Yes, of course. Thank you for
              calling and bringing this to my
              attention.
                    (beat)
              No, I appreciate the seriousness.
              Trust me.
                    (beat)
              Yes, I too, would like to see this
              resolved with extreme prejudice. I
              agree.
                    (beat)
              Right. I'll meet you there.

Raleigh slams the phone down.

INT. FBI HEADQUARTERS - SAME TIME

Greg rushes down the hall to the office he shares with JD.

He rushes into the office, where JD sits at a desk reading a report.

>   GREG
>   The crap is hitting the fan.

>   JD
>   Finally, some action. What is it?

Greg walks to the cork board with all of the photos. Recent photos of all of the brothers have been added to the wall.

>   GREG
>   It turns out all of these guys are
>   actually brothers.

>   JD
>   No way.

>   GREG
>   Yeah. Haven't figured that one out
>   yet, the Russians just contacted
>   Raleigh and they don't sound happy.
>   They just set up a meet.

>   JD
>   Do we know the when and where?

>   GREG
>   We do.

INT. THE PALAZZO - ROOM CORRIDOR - DAY

The brothers exit their room and are walking from their suite to the elevator.

When the elevator arrives they all enter and turn to face the door.

MUSAK can be heard as they travel down.

INTERCUT THE FOLLOWING

INT. THE PALAZZO CASINO - SAME TIME

A group of ten pair of fine black leather shoes walk across the brightly colored, garish, carpet of the casino.

They walk from LEFT TO RIGHT.

These belong to Bruce, Sergi and the Russian mobsters.

INT. THE PALAZZO CASINO - SAME TIME

A new group of feet walk from RIGHT TO LEFT.

There are two male pairs of shoes and one female -- this is obviously Raleigh, Geoffrey and Juliette.

INT. THE PALAZZO CASINO - SAME TIME

A third group of feet enter the casino and walk towards the CAMERA.

The shoes are comfortable, practical, leather shoes, that scream 'FBI.'

INT. ELEVATOR - CONTINUOUS

The brothers are completely unaware that all forces are converging on them as they ride the elevator down to the casino level.

They stand silently, listening to the MUSAK and watching the numbers count down the floors.

SPLIT SCREEN - THE FEET OF BRUCE AND THE RUSSIANS

SPLIT SCREEN INTO THIRDS - THE FEET OF RALEIGH, GEOFFREY AND JULIETTE

SPLIT SCREEN INTO FOURTHS - THE FEET OF THE FBI AGENTS

A final DING of the elevator as it reaches the casino floor and the doors open.

INT. CASINO AT ELEVATOR DOOR - CONTINUOUS

As the elevator doors open to revel the four brothers, the Russians and Raleigh and his group, all converge at the same time and place.

Greg, JD and other FBI agents hold back to see what happens.

The brothers are completely surprised and are about to put up a fight until the Russians subtly place guns into their ribs.

The brothers are lead from the casino.

The FBI agents follow behind discretely.

EXT. NEVADA DESERT - DAY

Four large black SUVs pull up in the desert.

The front doors open and Sergi exits one vehicle along with others that look just like him. It is like a gathering of mutant Slovakian clones wearing tight black T-shirts, black jeans and glasses with crew cuts and Russian prison tattoos.

The bodyguards proceed to open the back doors of the SUV where the brothers are roughly pulled out of the cars and dropped into the dirt.

Raleigh exits one vehicle with Geoffrey and Juliette.

Standing in the desert already are more Russian bodyguards with Bruce and Lev. In front of them is Pete.

The brothers are pushed toward Pete who hugs them when they all converge.

                    KELLY
          How you doin' little bro?

                    PETE
          I'm sorry Kelly. I tried not to
          tell them --

                    KELLY
          Don't worry about it. I'm sorry I
          got you into this in the first
          place.

                    BRUCE
          This is a wonderful family reunion,
          but there are more important things
          to discuss here. Like, where the
          hell our money is...

                    KELLY
          We used it to buy the code
          remember?

                    BRUCE
          I do. And I had that code checked,
          it's as bogus as the crap you sold
          Raleigh. Again, using our money.

                    RALEIGH
          You little shits. I'm going to kill
          all of you.

                    KELLY
          Like you did our father?

                    RALEIGH
          What? Who? Right. I haven't the
          foggiest who your bloody father is.

                    HARRISON
          Frank Russell ring any bells?

                    RALEIGH
          Frank Russell? You lot all belong
          to Frank? Oh, that is rich.

                    BRUCE
          Raleigh did you off their dad?

                    RALEIGH
          Well...yeah. He had it coming
          though.

                    KELLY
          Why because you are a crappy
          businessman and you couldn't please
          your woman?

Juliette smiles.

Raleigh notices.

                    RALEIGH
               (to Juliette)
          What are you on about? You can join
          them you know.

                    JULIETTE
          What?

                    RALEIGH
          Yeah. I know about your little
          liaison with pretty boy over there.
          Keeping it in the family, were you?

                    JULIETTE
          You bastard.

Juliette slaps Raleigh.

Bruce and the Russians are enjoying this actually.

> RALEIGH
> Save it. Get over there with the
> lot of them.

Geoffrey pushes Juliette over to where the brothers are
standing.

> KELLY
> You really are high class Raleigh.

> RALEIGH
> Oh sod off.

> BRUCE
> Enough. While I respect the honor
> in what you tried, I could care
> less. Where is our money?

Kelly takes a step forward.

> KELLY
> Listen --

He is summarily punched in the stomach by Sergi.

> BRUCE
> No you listen. You have one minute
> to tell us where you put the money
> and then we are going to kill you.

> HARRISON
> (to Kelly)
> So far I think this is going really
> well for us.

Kelly gives Harrison a dirty look, or at least the best he
can considering he is on his knees holding his stomach
gasping for air to return to his lungs.

> HARRISON (CONT'D)
> Let me handle this from here. Okay?

Kelly nods his agreement.

> RALEIGH
> Let me just kill them. Geoffrey.

Raleigh motions for Geoffrey to shoot them.

Geoffrey steps forward and unholsters his gun.

Sergi and his clones draw their weapons.

Everyone stops and all of the brothers raise their hands in
the air.

                    BRUCE
          Hold on there, Quick Draw. If there
          is going to be any killing we will
          do it after we have our money back.

                    HARRISON
          We can get your money for you. But
          what's the point if you're just
          going to kill us anyway?

                    BRUCE
          To die more quickly. What's better
          a bullet in the back of the head,
          or a beat down by the Russian Gulag
          Gang.
               (to Russians)
          No offense boys.

The Russian's all nod approvingly.

                    HARRISON
          Those are our only choices?

                    BRUCE
          What did you expect guys? You stole
          from us twice. You think we should
          just forgive and forget?

                    HARRISON
          If you want your money, you have to
          ask Raleigh for it.

                    RALEIGH
          I gave you all the money I received
          from them. You should know --

                    HARRISON
          Sure you gave it back to us, but
          technically we gave it back again.

                    RALEIGH
          What?

                    BRUCE
          What?

                    HARRISON
          Raleigh hasn't made payments on his
          casino for the past few months.
               (MORE)

                    HARRISON (CONT'D)
          He has been stalling the bank and
          his other debtors with promises of
          better things.

                    BRUCE
          So what?

                    HARRISON
          So, the bank was more than happy to
          accept anyone who would assume the
          responsibility for the bad debt,
          especially in this economy.

                    KELLY
          We made up the payments and assumed
          control of The Palace.

                    RALEIGH
          You what?

                    KELLY
          It's true. So technically --
                    (to Bruce)
          You are the proud new owner of his
          casino.

                    RALEIGH
          Brilliant. We were planning on
          working together anyway, you can
          just --

                    BRUCE
          No so fast Raleigh.

                    RALEIGH
          But...

                    BRUCE
          You guys are pretty smart.

                    KELLY
          Smart enough to save our lives?

                    BRUCE
          I doubt it. I need a minute to
          think.

                    KELLY
          Hey, take all the time you want.

Bruce turns to speak with Lev in whispered tones. The two
talk for a moment and then Bruce turns back to the group.

                    BRUCE
     So you are telling me, our money is
     tied up in his casino?

                    HARRISON
     Yes.

                    RALEIGH
     That is great, we can --

                    BRUCE
     -- Shut up, Raleigh. You have
     turned out to be the entire cause
     of all of the problems here.

                    RALEIGH
     How do you see that?

                    BRUCE
     Let's see, first you killed their
     old man for some reason. Then you
     come to us because you can't keep
     your casino running so you concoct
     some online scheme that is supposed
     to fix everything, but I suspect
     that under your guidance it will
     suck and fail as well --

                    PETE
     Well, actually --

                    HARRISON
     Pete, shut up. Now is not the time
     to defend your program.

                    BRUCE
     Speaking of which, where is the
     program? Is there even one that
     works?

                    KELLY
     Yes and we have it.

                    BRUCE
     So let me get this straight, you
     guys come along, basically just to
     jack with Raleigh for some revenge
     trip --
          (to brothers)
     Am I right?

The brothers all nod in agreement.

                         BRUCE (CONT'D)
          And we are caught in the middle.
                    (to Raleigh)
          I am half tempted to let these guys
          go, take possession of your casino,
          and leave you here in the desert.

                         GEOFFREY
          Can I work for you guys?

                         RALEIGH
          What? You wanker!

                         GEOFFREY
          Honestly Raleigh you are a bit of a
          prat.

                         LEV
          Bruce, I am beginning to think it
          would just be easiest to kill all
          of them.

Just then a number of helicopters appear and more black SUVs,
these with police light bars flashing.

The Russians point their weapons at the new intruders.

The brothers hit the ground.

Kelly grabs Juliette and pulls her to the ground making sure
she is safe.

Raleigh and Geoffrey kneel down under the prop wash from the
helicopters.

                         AGENT IN HELICOPTER (O.S.)
          Drop your weapons and get on the
          ground!

The black SUVs speed up. Dirt thrown in the air from the
tires.

FBI tactical team along with Agents Greg and JD leap out with
weapons drawn.

They look at the helicopters and at each other.

                         JD
          Who they hell ordered air support?

                         GREG
          It's not us.

Operators free repel from the helicopters.

The Russians are surrounded.

Wisely they dropped their guns and raised their hands.

Everyone looks around confused.

The FBI tactical team shouts at the Russians, the brothers,
Raleigh and Geoffrey as well as the other tactical team of
unknown operators, who are likewise shouting at everyone.

Basically, mass confusion with a lot of guns being pointed at
everyone.

                    PETE
          I think I have to pee.

                    TYCE
          Now is not the time for a potty
          break.

                    PETE
          Too late.

Once the Russians are flat on the ground with their arms and
legs spread, and the helicopters have landed, Agent's JD and
Greg approach the other team of operators.

They are greeted with the business end of the assault weapons
the operators are carrying.

JD and Greg hold up their credentials.

                    JD
          Whoa! Whoa! FBI! Put down your
          guns!

The brothers stay flat on the ground watching all of the
controlled mayhem around them.

                    HARRISON
          Did you arrange this?

                    KELLY
          Thanks for the credit bro, I may
          have been in contact with the FBI
          but I lost control when you made
          your announcement.

Stepping from the helicopter, dressed in black fatigues and
military boots, is NSA agent DAN FOSTER.

He approaches the scene and Agents JD and Greg.

                    DAN FOSTER
          That won't be necessary.

                    JD
          Who the hell are you?

                    DAN FOSTER
          Dan Foster, NSA. This is our
          operation.

                    JD
          Says you. We've been tracking these
          Russians for months now and we
          finally have something that will
          stick.

                    DAN FOSTER
          Good for you. We've had our agent
          in deep cover with them for two
          years, tracking them from Moscow to
          Chicago, to Vegas. This is a matter
          of national security and we have
          jurisdiction. Have your agents
          holster their weapons and stand
          down. I will let you know, when and
          if you are needed.

Foster walks away from Agents JD and Greg and approaches
Bruce who lays on the ground with his hands on his head.

Foster reaches down and offers a hand to Bruce.

Bruce accepts and stands up, brushing the dirt from his
tailored suit.

                    DAN FOSTER
          Fine work agent. Looks like we
          arrived just in time.

                    BRUCE
          Thank you sir. I'm glad you
          received my message.

                    DAN FOSTER
          Job well done. I bet you will be
          glad this operation is finished.

                    BRUCE
          You have no idea.

Lev looks up at Bruce.

                    LEV
          You son of a --

One of the NSA operators pushes Lev's head back into the dirt
before he can finish.

                    DAN FOSTER
          We'll clean up from here.

                    BRUCE
          Thank you sir.
             (beat)
          Sir? What about them?

Bruce points to the brothers.

                    DAN FOSTER
          The US government could give a
          shaved rat's ass about them. Cut
          them loose.

                    BRUCE
          Yes sir.

                    JD
          Wait a minute. We have an ongoing
          investigation that they are
          involved in.

Bruce approaches JD and Greg.

                    BRUCE
             (whispering)
          C'mon guys. These guys are nobody.
          They just solved a murder which you
          can claim credit for and even
          served up the killer on a plater.
          He just confessed and I can testify
          to that.
             (beat)
          Listen, we'll take the Russians,
          that's what we care about, you take
          Raleigh and his bodyguard. What do
          you say we cut these guys a break
          and let them go?

EXT. HR OFFICE AT THE PALACE - DAY

The office door reads HR department.

INT. THE PALACE CASINO - DAY

A well dressed man walks through The Palace casino. He has an
ear piece in his ear.

As a uniformed security guard passes the man, they acknowledge each other.

Finally the man turns and it is: Daniel.

FREEZE FRAME on Daniel. SUPER: "Daniel, head of security for the palace hotel and casino."

As ACTION resumes, Daniel speaks into a lapel microphone.

> DANIEL
> How's the eye in the sky?

INT. SECURITY MONITORING ROOM - DAY

Inside a dimly lit room, a wall of monitors show every angle of the hotel as seen from the security cameras posted in the ceiling.

Tyce turns -- FREEZE FRAME on Tyce. SUPER: "Tyce, director of video surveillance."

As ACTION resumes, Tyce speaks into a walkie talkie:

> TYCE
> The all seeing eye is awake and
> vigilant. I think it's time. See
> you there.

INT. THE PALACE COMPUTER ROOM - DAY

IT staff are working on the servers that control all of the casino operations.

One staff member in particular helps the others. He is obviously in charge.

The staff member turns and it is: Pete.

FREEZE FRAME on Pete. SUPER: "Pete, the head of it and internet security."

As ACTION resumes a CHIME goes off on Pete's tablet and he opens the message window to see an event reminder.

> PETE
> (to staff)
> Got to go.

INT. GRAND BALLROOM AT THE PALACE - DAY

Inside a palatial theater ballroom, preparation are being made for what looks like a huge party.

Balloons are placed in various spots, lights are being checked, the sound system is being tested.

People move around quickly everywhere.

One man in particular seems to be the center of everyone's attention and he is directing all of the workers.

When he turns it is: Harrison.

FREEZE FRAME on Harrison. SUPER: "Harrison, vice president of events and entertainment."

As ACTION resumes Harrison's cell phone rings and he answers it.

> HARRISON
> Harrison. Is it time already? Okay.

INT. WEDDING CHAPEL - LATER

A bride and groom stand at the alter.

She is dressed in a simple, yet lovely white designer outfit -- not a wedding dress.

He wears a dark suit and tie.

As the door to the chapel opens the bride and groom turn and reveal:

FREEZE FRAME on Kelly and Juliette. SUPER: "Kelly and Juliette became joint owners in the palace hotel / casino and online gaming portal. They are about to become husband and wife."

As ACTION resumes, all of the brothers enter the chapel.

Everyone is happy and smiling.

> KELLY
> Glad you guys could join us.

One final guest enters the chapel and waves to Kelly.

It is Steve Wynn.

INT. BAR INSIDE THE PALACE - LATER

The ceremony over, the brothers and Juliette have gathered at a private table at the bar within The Palace.

Ties have been loosened and jackets thrown over the backs of their chairs.

A WAITRESS delivers a round of drinks.

Once she leaves Kelly raises his glass in a toast.

                KELLY
       To sweet revenge.

                PETE
       To a new patent worth a billion
       dollars!

                DANIEL
       To our own casino.

                TYCE
       To success and new beginnings.

                JULIETTE
       To new friends.

                HARRISON
       To family.

                ALL BROTHERS
       Cheers!

The group all take a drink.

A young attractive girl approaches the brother's table. VALERIE is the personification of confidence and no bullshit.

When she reaches the table, Pete tries to hit on her -- his first attempt to talk to a girl, using what he learned from Kelly.

                PETE
       Well hello. I'm Pete, what's your
       name?

                VALERIE
       Not my type --

The other brothers all react to Pete being shot down so abruptly.

Pete shrinks in his chair.

Valerie takes the drink from in front of him and throws it
back in one gulp.

                    KELLY
          I'm afraid I can't let you shoot
          down my bro and his drink like
          that.

                    VALERIE
          I'm here for sentimental reasons.

                    KELLY
          Such as?

                    VALERIE
          Name's Valerie Russell. I believe
          you filed a patent with Frank
          Russell's name on it. I'm here to
          collect my share of the profits.
          I'm sentimental about money and I
          since you are my brothers --

FREEZE FRAME ON brothers reaction.

                                        FADE TO BLACK.

LOGLINE

When Murphy's Law goes into full effect the day of David Swanson's biggest job interview, he must overcome multiple challenges in the New York subway system including mistaken identity as one of New York's most wanted criminals, or risk losing his girlfriend and dream job.

The Longest Subway Ride
by
Douglas King & William G. Phillips

FADE IN

EXT. NEW YORK CITY - DAY

DAVID SWANSON (27) struggles to carry several reusable bags
of groceries down a Manhattan street.

David is fresh, pressed and ready for success. A college
grad, with an Express store wardrobe, a fifty dollar haircut
and an eye on the career fast-track.

When he reaches the front door of his apartment building, he
accidentally drops a bag as he struggles to find his keys and
open the door.

                    DAVID
          Crap!

INT. APARTMENT BUILDING - CONTINUOUS

David nears the door of his apartment.

The PHONE RINGS inside.

He hurries to open the door. In the process dropping more of
his groceries on the floor.

                    DAVID
          Oh c'mon!

INT. STUDIO APARTMENT - CONTINUOUS

The door swings open.

David drops his grocery bags and runs for the phone, crushing
a bag of potato chips with his foot in the process.

Thankfully it only takes two steps to reach the other side of
an apartment this small so reaching the phone in one is no
problem.

                    DAVID
          Please be Overend. Please be
          Overend.

David picks up the phone. It is SANDY from his apartment
management.

                    DAVID
          Hello?

                    SANDY
          David Swanson?

                    DAVID
          Yes.

                    SANDY (O.S.)
          This is Sandy at Bettino Equities.

                    DAVID
          Yes.

Disappointed. He collapses onto his bed.

                    SANDY (O.S.)
          We have received your letter
          regarding the $537 expense from the
          move-in last week.

                    DAVID
          Uh-huh.

David listens while he flips on the television. It is barely
audible amid the phone conversation.

                    SANDY (O.S.)
          This is to inform you that your
          request for reimbursement has been
          denied.

                    DAVID
          Denied? What do you mean? My door
          had no locks. You don't provide
          locks on the door?

                    SANDY (O.S.)
          Of course we do, Mr. Swanson.
          However, as we discussed, you
          failed to follow proper procedure
          as outlined in your tenant's
          handbook.

                    DAVID
          But I didn't receive my tenant's
          handbook until yesterday.

                    SANDY (O.S.)
          That's not our problem.

                    DAVID
            (growing increasingly
             irritated)
          You mailed it to me!

                    SANDY (O.S.)
          Mr. Swanson, I don't have time for
          your ranting.
                      (MORE)

                    SANDY (O.S.) (CONT'D)
          As far as we're concerned, this
          matter is resolved. Your account
          will be billed a $30 processing
          fee.

                    DAVID
          Processing fee? What are you
          talking about?

                    SANDY (O.S.)
          Your tenant's handbook clearly
          states that matters of
          reimbursement are subject to a
          processing fee.

                    DAVID
          Tenant's hand...You can't do that!
          This isn't the Soviet Union.

                    SANDY (O.S.)
          No, but it is New York. Good day.

Sandy hangs up.

David leans back on the bed. Stunned.

                    DAVID
          Welcome to New York.

David gets up and begins putting away his groceries.

The PHONE RINGS again.

David grabs it. Takes a deep breath. Has to calm himself.
Answers.

                    DAVID
          Hello?

                    ASSISTANT
          David Swanson?

                    DAVID
          Yes.

                    ASSISTANT
          Please hold for Deputy Mayor
          Michael Overend.

                    DAVID
          Yes, of course.

A CLICK.

Pause.

CLICK.

>   MICHAEL OVEREND
>   David!

>   DAVID
>   Mr. Deputy Mayor, it's a pleasure
>   to speak with you.

>   MICHAEL OVEREND
>   We have received your resume and
>   portfolio. And I must say, we're
>   quite impressed.

>   DAVID
>   Thank you.

>   MICHAEL OVEREND
>   I have one concern, however. Part
>   of your background is in
>   advertising. We do no ad stuff
>   here. It's strictly PR.

>   DAVID
>   I realize that, sir. In fact,
>   that's one of the reasons I'm so
>   interested in the position.
>   Advertising has been good to me,
>   but PR is where my heart is.

>   MICHAEL OVEREND
>   What else would a PR guy say?

>   DAVID
>   Exactly.

>   MICHAEL OVEREND
>   What I need is someone who can make
>   mass layoffs sound like increased
>   vacation time. Is that you?

>   DAVID
>   Are you kidding? I could sell a cat
>   to a rat.

>   MICHAEL OVEREND
>   I like your style. Let's meet.

>   DAVID
>   Great.

                    MICHAEL OVEREND
When are you available? I can be
flexible.

                    DAVID
How about Friday?

                    MICHAEL OVEREND
Friday is no good. I can meet you
today.

                    DAVID
Today?

                    MICHAEL OVEREND
Four o'clock.

                    DAVID
Ah. Four o'clock. Sure. Four
o'clock is fine.

                    MICHAEL OVEREND
See you then.

                    DAVID
Where?

                    MICHAEL OVEREND
City Hall, room four-twleve.

                    DAVID
City Hall, of course. Okay, great.

                    MICHAEL OVEREND
See you then.

Michael hangs up.

David pumps his fist in the air. <u>Victory!</u>

                    DAVID
Yes! Mayor's office, here I come.

The television can now be heard.

                    TELEVISION BROADCASTER
These are the only known pictures
of the so-called subway Mole-Man.

David turns his attention to the television.

On display are several blurry pictures of what looks like a
dirty, unshaven, homeless man.

David turns up the volume with the remote control.

                    TELEVISION BROADCASTER
          These photos, of course, were taken
          more than a year ago. Mr. Merritt,
          who claims to have seen the Mole-
          Man in the Union Square 4,5,6
          subway tunnel late last night, says
          the man looks very much the same,
          except for the beard. The
          sanitation department, along with
          police, are now launching an all-
          out search for the Mole-Man, who
          has been accused of crimes ranging
          from robbery to murder. He's been
          on the run for more than nine years
          and is said to be extremely
          dangerous. If you have any
          information...

David MUTES the television with the remote.

                    DAVID
          What a weird city.

David looks at a clock on the wall.

IT'S 10 AM.

David fiddles with some papers near the phone and dials a
number.

INTERCUT - INT. NEW YORK OFFICE BUILDING - NEWSROOM/STUDIO
APARTMENT

The phone on a small desk in a cubicle is RINGING.

NATALIE FARMER (27), beat reporter charm with the looks of a
runway model, answers the phone.

The hustle and bustle of a newspaper office behind her.

Natalie is keeping an eye on several co-workers watching a
television in front of her.

                    NATALIE
          Metro.

                    DAVID
          Nat, it's me.

                    NATALIE
          Me who?

                    DAVID
Come on, Nat, you know who.

                    NATALIE
Oh yeah, now I recognize the voice.
It's the guy who stood me up last
night.

                    DAVID
You know darn well I didn't stand
you up. I told you I couldn't make
it.

                    NATALIE
You said you'd probably be there.

                    DAVID
Probably. That's the key.

                    NATALIE
I see. Probably in Davespeak means
probably not.

                    DAVID
I didn't think it was a big deal.

                    NATALIE
No, it wasn't. Like my dad said, I
probably don't want to be with
someone who doesn't want to meet my
parents anyway.

                    DAVID
I will meet them. I just couldn't
last night.

                    NATALIE
I understand. Drinking with old
college buddies is much more
important.

                    DAVID
I hadn't seen them in years. Well,
since college.

                    NATALIE
I said I understand.

                    DAVID
Yes, and you were so sincere. Look,
I'm sorry. I honestly thought it
didn't matter to you if I came.
With me living here now, I can meet
your parents any time.
                    (MORE)

                    DAVID (CONT'D)
         (beat)
    Tell you what, I owe you one.

                    NATALIE
    A big one.

                    DAVID
    Listen. I have great news.

                    NATALIE
    The mayor's office called?

                    DAVID
    Yep.

                    NATALIE
    That's great. Congratulations.

                    DAVID
    Thanks. Only one problem.

                    NATALIE
    You can't meet tonight.

                    DAVID
    How do you...Unless you can do it
    later. My interview is today.

                    NATALIE
    I can't. I'm here 'til at least ten
    tonight. I have to come back to
    cover a press conference at seven.
    It's that Mole-Man thing.

                    DAVID
    Did they catch him?

                    NATALIE
    Not yet, but I hear they're closing
    in.

                    DAVID
    That whole thing's just weird.

                    NATALIE
    Well, get used to it, hon. You live
    in New York now. You'll hear crazy
    things every day.

                    DAVID
    Especially with you around.

                    NATALIE
          Maybe we can meet for lunch. I
          could probably sneak out of here
          for an hour.

                    DAVID
          Where?

                    NATALIE
          Billy's? Corner of Broadway and
          Chambers. You can walk to your
          interview from there.

                    DAVID
          Okay, one-thirty work?

                    NATALIE
          Yeah. See you then.

                    DAVID
          Hey.

                    NATALIE
          What?

                    DAVID
          I really do want to meet your
          parents. I'm sorry about last
          night.

                    NATALIE
          You'll make it up to me. Got to go.

INT. STUDIO APARTMENT

David pulls out a white dress shirt from the closet.

He UN-MUTES the television again.

A DOCTOR is being interviewed.

                    DOCTOR
          Underground dwellers should be
          treated just like animals. Once
          someone goes underground, they lose
          all sense of civilization. If you
          come across the Mole-Man, you
          should not try to talk to or feed
          him. Our psychological profiles
          show that he is extremely
          dangerous.

David turns on the iron sitting on the mini-ironing board set
up on the coffee table.

As the iron heats and he listens to the television, he puts on his pants.

He pulls out a subway map of Manhattan and lays it on the board.

He looks for the remote, then reaches across the coffee table to grab it. In the process the iron falls onto the map and it starts to smolder.

He turns off the television with the remote. Then realizes --

                    DAVID
          Oh crap!

He starts tapping the map with his hand and is able to stop the burning.

A part of the map is charred, but it didn't burn completely. David holds it up and attempts to read it.

                    DAVID
          Great! I just fried a quarter of
          Manhattan. Ah, it's always the part
          you need.

Just then, the smoke detector SHRIEKS.

                    DAVID
          Crap!

He jumps onto the couch, rips the cover off the detector and disconnects the battery. It stops BEEPING.

                    DAVID
          Wonder how much I'll be charged for
          that?

Back to the map.

                    DAVID
          City Hall. City Hall.
              (beat)
          Okay, I'm here.

He points to the East 90s with his left hand.

He begins to iron with his right.

                    DAVID
          And I need to get here.

He points to the southern tip of Manhattan, charred on the map.

He continues to iron.

> DAVID
> Looks like the 4,5,6 to City Hall.
> Easy enough. If I leave now I
> should have plenty of time.

He finishes ironing the shirt.

> DAVID
> The Sun is out. My shirt is wrinkle-
> free. And I have an interview with
> the mayor's office. I love this
> city.

INT. SUBWAY STATION--DAY

> DAVID
> I hate this city.

David is trying to put a $10 bill into a MTA MetroCard
vending machine, but the machine keeps rejecting it.

After several tries, he pulls out his wallet again.

He is looking for a crisp bill but can only find a bunch of
old ATM receipts.

Finally, David takes the $10 bill and tries to flatten it out
the best he can.

A line is forming behind him with less than patient, tolerant
or understanding people. It's New York.

He looks over his shoulder and smiles nervously.

He again inserts the bill into the machine and it is again
rejected before it goes halfway.

He takes the bill and rubs it on the corner of the machine to
get the wrinkles out.

> IMPATIENT MAN
> Come on!

David takes the bill once again and inserts it into the
machine.

This time it is accepted all the way.

He turns to the line that has formed and smiles proudly.

The machine WHIRS for a moment then rejects his bill.

David kicks the token dispenser.

> IMPATIENT MAN
> Get out of the way you pecker-wood!
> You'll make us miss our train!

The kicking and shouting get the attention of a POLICE
OFFICER nearby. He is watching David now.

> DAVID
> Give me a second. I'll miss the
> train too, you know.

> IMPATIENT MAN
> Nobody gives a rat's ass if you
> miss the train.

> DAVID
> (to self)
> Nice.

> IMPATIENT MAN
> What'd you say?

David inserts the bill again.

It is accepted, the machine WHIRS and a pile of shredded
paper drops down into the token tray.

The machine has eaten his money.

> DAVID
> Ugh! Are you kidding me?!

> IMPATIENT MAN
> Move it buddy. I don't got all day!

> DAVID
> All right. One second.

David scoops the shreds of money and carries them over to the
token booth.

There is a line there as well.

David nervously checks his watch as a No. 6 train pulls into
the station.

TICKET OFFICE

The TICKET WOMAN is heavy-set women wearing far too much
makeup. While handing out MetroCards, she is reading a copy
of "Soap Opera Digest."

David dumps the pile of chewed-up and spat-out money into her tray and pushes it toward her under the glass.

> DAVID
> Excuse me? Hello? Your machine ate
> my money. Can I be reimbursed
> please?

Without looking up from her reading the woman pushes the money back to him.

> TICKET WOMAN
> Fill out a refund form.

David pushes the money back to her.

> DAVID
> And where would I get such a form?

Finally looking up from her magazine, and none to pleased about it either, the woman places a thick set of forms under the glass and pushes it to David.

The forms barely can squeeze out of the slot.

> TICKET WOMAN
> Fill out both sides and sign at all
> the X's. Then return it to me.

David checks his pockets.

> DAVID
> Pen?

The ticket woman gives a frustrated look, then slides a pen to him.

> DAVID
> Thank you. You've been ever so
> kind.

Ticket woman returns to her reading after giving David a wise smile.

David places the form against the glass of the ticket office and begins to fill it out.

Ticket woman looks up when she realizes what he is doing and TAPs on the glass.

> TICKET WOMAN
> Not here.

She motions him away.

                         TICKET WOMAN
                Next. Step up.

David steps in front of the woman moving up in line.

                         DAVID
                And where do you propose that I do
                fill it out?

                         TICKET WOMAN
                I don't care. On the subway.

                         DAVID
                But I can't get on the subway until
                I get my refund, now can I?

                         TICKET WOMAN
                There's no loitering at the token
                booth.
                    (beat)
                Next.

                         DAVID
                I'm not loitering. I'm filling out
                a form.

The woman behind David has now pushed her way in front of
him. She slides her money under the glass.

David turns around to see a line of about ten people waiting.

All are frustrated with him.

                         DAVID
                I don't have to stand in line
                again, do I?

By now the police officer has made his way over to the ticket
office.

                         POLICE OFFICER
                Is there a problem here?

                         DAVID
                No offi --

                         TICKET WOMAN
                Yes, this man is becoming hostile.

                         DAVID
                I am not!

                         TICKET WOMAN
                See.

                         POLICE OFFICER
           Sir, I'm going to have to ask you
           to step away from the booth.

                         DAVID
           Fine, fine. I just want my refund.
           My money was destroyed by the token
           machine, that's all. I don't think
           that's too much to ask.

David walks over to the nearest wall and begins to fill out
the form.

The police officer walks away but continues to watch David
very closely.

David goes through the form and finds that it asks all sorts
of questions that are not pertinent to the situation. He
READS THE FORM OUT LOUD and becomes more exasperated as he
reads.

                         DAVID
           Mother's maiden name? Why on Earth
           do they need that? Place of
           employment? Years of education?
           This is absurd.

He continues to fill out the form, then hears the EXPRESS
TRAIN BUZZER.

He is going to miss the next train if he doesn't hurry.

David speeds up and fills out the form hastily.

There are at least ten pages to the form. Front and back. By
the time he has reached the seventh page he is completely
exasperated.

He finishes the form and returns to the token booth, where
the line has dwindled.

The ticket woman is back to reading her magazine and ignores
him when he first walks up.

                         DAVID
           Excuse me? Excuse me? Hi, remember
           me? Here's your form. May I please
           have my refund? I'm in a bit of a
           hurry.

Ticket woman takes the form and slowly and deliberately flips
through each page.

David is becoming increasingly more impatient.

                 DAVID
      Could you please hurry?

Ticket woman stops on one of the pages and pushes it back
under the window.

               TICKET WOMAN
      You forgot to sign here. Line one-
      twenty-seven.

               DAVID
      My God, woman, you have my
      signature in seventy-two other
      places on the document. Missing one
      really matters?

               TICKET WOMAN
      If you want your money it matters.

David signs and pushes it back through to the ticket woman.

               DAVID
      There. Now can you please hurry?
      I'm going to miss the train.

               TICKET WOMAN
      Oh, don't worry. You've already
      missed that train.

David gives a sarcastic smile.

Ticket woman slowly goes through the rest of the form and,
once she is satisfied that it has been filled out properly,
puts it down and picks up her phone.

               DAVID
      Excuse me. Ma'am? What are you
      doing?

               TICKET WOMAN
      I have to call it in. I can't give
      you a refund without approval.

               DAVID
      Yes, I think you can. We're talking
      about ten bucks here. Please, just
      give me six tokens and a buck and
      I'll be on my way.

               TICKET WOMAN
      Rules are rules. They are there for
      a reason, you know.

                         DAVID
              I don't have time for this. Look,
              keep the money.

                       TICKET WOMAN
              Hey wait!

But it is too late.

David jumps the turnstile.

He is running to catch the express that is pulling in.

The police officer sees him jump the turnstile and takes off
after him.

PLATFORM

David races down the steps, onto the platform, and runs after
the train.

He just barely makes it in the subway car before the doors
shut.

The police officer is too late.

INT. SUBWAY TRAIN

David looks out the window back at the officer and shrugs.

The police officer is pissed. He takes his walkie-talkie off
his belt and calls in (MOS).

The train pulls away from the platform.

David walks through the car looking for an open seat.

He spots an empty seat and sits down heavily. He sighs and
relaxes.

He stares out the window, growing bored and anxious, David
looks around for something to do.

Across from him is an elderly couple. Further down the car is
an Asian couple obviously on vacation. The other passengers
are various businessmen and -women. Nothing too unusual.

The elderly couple is watching him very intently as if they
are afraid of him. The woman clutches her purse tightly. They
hold a quiet conversation with each other.

                        OLD WOMAN
              Did you see the policeman chasing
              him?

                    OLD MAN
          That boy is bad news.

                    OLD WOMAN
          I bet he's a fugitive.

David smiles at them to ease the tension but that only makes
them more nervous.

                    DAVID
               (under his breath)
          Jeez, tough room.

David turns back to look out the window.

There is nothing to see but darkness and the occasional light
flashing by.

Growing bored, David reaches into his coat pocket for his
phone.

As he reaches into his pocket the old woman across from him
SCREAMS and the man yells...

                    OLD MAN
          He's got a gun!

This startles everyone in the car, including David.

All eyes turn to David.

The Asian man snaps a picture.

David is confused as to whom the old woman could be referring
to and quickly ducks for cover.

When David turns back to face the old couple, the woman is
pointing a can of pepper spray at him.

                    OLD WOMAN
          Don't move, mister. I've got you
          covered!

                    DAVID
          What? Are you nuts?

                    OLD MAN
          Don't try anything son, she's a
          dead aim.

                    OLD WOMAN
          Now take your hand out of your
          pocket nice and slow.

                         DAVID
              Lady, you've been watching too many
              cop shows.

David begins to remove his hand from his coat.

                         DAVID
              I'm trying to find my phone. Here,
              let me show you.

David begins to rustle through his coat again and this scares
the old couple.

No one else in the train really cares anymore. Some have gone
back to what they were reading while others are watching or
moving to other cars.

                         OLD MAN
              Blast him, honey, he's going for
              his piece!

The old woman gives David a LONG BURST OF PEPPER SPRAY.

It hits David square in the face and he begins to SCREAM.

As he pulls his hands from his coat to cover his face, his
cellular phone falls to the ground.

In unison, the couple look down at the phone that has fallen
on the floor. Then to each other. Then to David.

They realize what they have done...

                         OLD MAN
                    (to wife)
              Run.

The couple quickly gather their belongings and run from the
car into a different car to get away from David.

David is still clutching his face and screaming.

                         DAVID
              Really?

David rubs his eyes, then takes a handkerchief out of his
pocket to wipe some of the spray from his face.

It takes some time but, finally, the stinging goes away and
David can see.

His hair is now disheveled and his eyes are bloodshot.

As David looks around, he sees that everyone is ignoring him completely. Not one person comes to help him.

The subway car comes to a screeching halt, and the lights flicker then go out.

                    DAVID
          Gaaaa! What now?

David sits in the dark for a moment. He is growing impatient.

                    TRAIN CONDUCTOR (O.S.)
          Ladies and gentleman, due to an
          electrical outage at 23rd Street,
          we've lost power on this track. Due
          to the loss of overhead lighting,
          for your safety we ask that you
          please be patient and stay put. We
          should be moving shortly.

There are GROANS in the cabin.

Frustrated, David looks down at his watch.

It is 10:45.

                    DAVID
          So much having plenty of time.

WATCH FACE

It is now 11:15.

INT. SUBWAY CAR

David is looking down at his watch.

Over the LOUD SPEAKER:

                    TRAIN CONDUCTOR (O.S.)
          Ladies and gentleman, we apologize
          for the continuing delay. Please be
          patient. We should be moving
          shortly.

                    DAVID
          Come on.

WATCH FACE

It is now 11:45.

SUBWAY CAR

David is growing more agitated with every passing second.

> DAVID
> What the hell is going on? We'll be
> moving shortly. Right.

The other people in the car continue to ignore David.

The man with the camera takes another picture of David even
though it is pitch black in the car.

> DAVID
> Would you kindly stop doing that?

The man takes another photo.

> DAVID
> I said stop it!

David has had enough.

He walks menacingly toward the man. With each step, the man
takes another photo. There is a strobing effect inside the
train car as David stalks his prey.

As David approaches he notices something outside the window
of the car.

He stops. Turns to look.

David sees a red-lit sign that reads: DOWNTOWN TUNNEL B. The
light flickers a little.

> TRAIN CONDUCTOR (O.S.)
> Ladies and gentleman, we're still
> working on the problem. Please
> remain patient. We'll be moving
> shortly.

> DAVID
> Yeah, whatever. I'll find my own
> way off this God-forsaken vehicle.
> Goodbye suckers.

David rushes over to the doors and attempts to pry them open.

The man takes another photo of David.

David turns and snarls at the man. David is losing his
composure.

It takes a little effort, but finally David is able to pry open the doors.

He jumps down from the subway car.

He slips a little and falls to one knee, dirtying his suit.

> DAVID
> Crap!

David turns back to the subway car and is just about to say something.

Just then, the lights turn back on and the car begins to slowly move away.

> DAVID
> Hey!
> (beat)
> Hey!

The sliding doors that David just pried open slam shut.

The man with the camera comes to the window and snaps another picture of David, who is now jogging next to the train desperately trying to get back in.

> DAVID
> Hey, open the door! Do you
> understand? Open the door!

The man takes another picture.

> DAVID
> Put your stupid camera down and
> open the door!

But it is too late.

The subway train is beginning to pick up speed and David cannot keep up.

He stops running and watches in total shock as the subway train pulls away from him. To add insult to injury, as the train passes by David sees the old man and woman looking out at him.

INT. SUBWAY CAR

> OLD WOMAN
> A nice boy.

> OLD MAN
> Fine young gentleman.

INT. SUBWAY TUNNEL

                    DAVID
          You old farts!

David watches the subway train disappear into the darkness.

                    DAVID
          Great. Just great.
               (beat)
          Now what?

David turns and walks back to the sign he saw earlier.

SUBWAY SERVICE TUNNEL

David looks into the narrow service tunnel with disgust.

                    DAVID
          This is wonderful, David, you're on
          your way to the most important
          interview of your young life and
          you screw it up. Get yourself lost
          in the bowels of New York City. And
          if there is any city you don't want
          to be in the bowels of it would be
          New York.

David makes his way down the dark service tunnel in the hopes of finding another downtown train.

He walks in darkness, feeling his way as he goes and making noises of disgust as his hands run over cold, wet things that he can only imagine.

After a short time, he sees a light ahead.

David speeds up as he nears the light. He is jogging, then running.

David reaches the end of the tunnel and walks into the light.

INT. SUBWAY STATION

A different subway station. A subway train.

The familiar closing door bell CHIME.

David jumps on the train.

INT. SUBWAY CAR

Making his way through the car, which is about half full, David finds a seat in an empty three-seat row near the door.

After a minute of traveling, the train pulls into a station.

The doors opens.

> CONDUCTOR (O.C.)
> Lexington Avenue.

A few people board.

A BUSINESSMAN sits down beside David.

The doors close.

> CONDUCTOR (O.C.)
> Next stop: Queens Plaza.

David is surprised.

> DAVID
> Queens Plaza? What train am I on?

Looking around for a sign.

> BUSINESSMAN
> What train am I on? What train am I
> on? My brother, you are not on any
> train. We are on a train.

The man speaks in a manner like Jesse Jackson. His voice
grows LOUDER.

> BUSINESSMAN
> That's right! We are together on
> this train, much like one
> brotherhood will cure this world of
> its ills.

David is not sure what to make of the man.

> BUSINESSMAN
> As long as we work together, it's
> the train to equal rights, it's the
> train to peace among men, it's the
> train to economic and social
> prosperity. This is the United
> States. The greatest country in all
> the world. And I should know--I've
> visited them all--Germany, Denmark,
> Philly . . .

> DAVID
> Yes, but is it the train to City
> Hall?

The man falls back to Earth.

                    BUSINESSMAN
          No, man, you want the 6. This is
          the N.

                    DAVID
          Thank you.

David shakes his head. <u>Can this day get any weirder</u>?

INT. SUBWAY STATION

The train enters a new station and stops.

David gets off.

David looks for a way to get to the other side of the track
to go back the way he came, but can't figure out how.

He approaches a TRANSIT OFFICER.

                    DAVID
          Excuse me. I got on the N in
          Manhattan going the wrong way. How
          do I get to the Manhattan-bound
          side?

                    TRANSIT OFFICER
          Exit and enter from the outside.

                    DAVID
          Yes, but -- and I'm kind of
          embarrassed -- I don't have any
          cash on me to buy another ticket on
          the other side.

                    TRANSIT OFFICER
          That's okay. Just tell the MTA
          clerk I said it was okay to let you
          through. I'll be here if she gives
          you any hassle.

                    DAVID
          Oh Thank you. I have been having
          the worst morning. I appreciate it.

EXT. CITY STREET - DAY

David exits the subway and sees an ATM at the State Federal
Bank adjacent to the main bank entrance.

INT. ATM - CONTINUOUS

David inserts his card and enters his PIN.

An error message appears on the screen.

                    DAVID
          What do you mean wrong PIN?

He enters it again. The machine takes it. David pushes a few
more buttons and the machine starts to WHIR.

Behind David, in the bank itself, THREE ARMED ROBBERS burst
in and begin waving guns at the tellers and customers.

Seeing this through the door that connects the two areas,
David panics.

                    DAVID
            Holy crap!

He wants to grab his money and run, but the machine is still
WHIRRING.

                    DAVID
            Come on.

The robbers inside have snatched up a few bags of money and,
much to David's dismay, exit through the ATM area.

As they walk past David, one of them stops and grabs his
money just as it appears from the machine.

                    DAVID
            Hey!

The robber stops, turns around, then grabs David's ATM card
as the machine spits it out.

                    ROBBER
            Wallet.

                    DAVID
            Huh?

                    ROBBER
          Give me your wallet. Now!

David hands over his wallet and the robber takes off out the
door.

                    DAVID
          I can't believe this.

David is not sure what to do.

Inside the bank, commotion reigns.

David picks up the phone at the ATM.

A TELLER comes on the other end.

                    TELLER (V.O)
          State Federal ATM Service. May I
          help you?

                    DAVID
          Yeah, I'd like to report my card
          stolen.

                    TELLER (V.O.)
          Okay, we should cancel the card
          right away.

                    DAVID
          Right, but what I really need is
          some cash.

                    TELLER (V.O.)
          Don't we all, sir?

                    DAVID
          No, you see, I am on my way to an
          interview. And my card was just
          stolen. And I need money to buy a
          subway token.
               (beat)
          Can't you tell the machine to give
          me some money and deduct it from my
          account?

                    TELLER (V.O.)
          I'm afraid not. I can only cancel
          the card. Would you like to do
          that?

                    DAVID
          Okay, sure.

                    TELLER (V.O.)
          What's the card number?

                    DAVID
          Card number? I don't have that.

                    TELLER (V.O.)
          Sir, I can't cancel your card
          without the number.

                    DAVID
          Yes, but the card was just stolen,
          so I don't have the number.

                    TELLER (V.O.)
          You don't have it written down in
          your wallet?

                    DAVID
          Well, no, it was stolen with the
          card. I was mugged. Get it?

                    TELLER (V.O.)
          I'm afraid I can't help you, sir.

                    DAVID
          Thank you so much. You have been a
          great help.

                    TELLER (V.O.)
          Your welcome sir, if you wouldn't
          mind staying on the line, I would
          like to transfer you to our
          customer satisfaction survey. It
          will just take a few minutes.

                    DAVID
          Are you serious?

                    TELLER (V.O.)
          These surveys help us to continue
          offering you the quality customer
          service you desire sir.

David slams the phone down.

David leaves the commotion of the bank.

EXT. CITY STREET - SAME

After walking across the street David walks down into the
subway again, on the Manhattan-bound side.

INT. SUBWAY STATION

He stops at the Ticket Office.

                    TICKET CLERK 2
          How many?

                    DAVID
          Yes, hi. I got on the wrong train
          in Manhattan. The nice officer over
          there...

David points to the other side of the track.

                    DAVID
          ...told me to just tell you that
          and you'd let me through the
          turnstiles.

                    TICKET CLERK 2
          Who told you that?

                    DAVID
          The officer over there.

David turns around to look for him. He spots him and points.

                    DAVID
          See him?

The ticket clerk looks.

The transit officer waves.

The ticket clerk nods her head affirmatively.

                    TICKET CLERK 2
          Go ahead. I'll buzz you through.

                    DAVID
          Thanks a lot.
               (to himself)
          Finally, some cooperation.

David turns around and walks toward the turnstile.

It BUZZES.

Just then, a TEENAGER jumps in front of David and goes
through the unlocked turnstile before David can.

The turnstile is locked again.

                    DAVID
          Really?

David returns to the ticket office and the clerk.

                    TICKET CLERK 2
          How many?

                    DAVID
          No, see, hi. It's still me.
          Somebody just jumped in front of
          me. I didn't get to go through.
          Could you buzz me again?

                         TICKET CLERK 2
                    You think I can give away free
                    rides all day?

                         DAVID
                    No, not at all. It's just that
                    someone jumped in front of me.

                         TICKET CLERK 2
                    You had your chance. Now you'll
                    have to pay. How many?

                         DAVID
                    Well, that's just it. I don't have
                    any money.

                         TICKET CLERK 2
                    Well then, it looks like you're out
                    of luck.
                         (beat)
                    Next. Step up.

A few people push David out of the way.

                         DAVID
                    I don't believe this.

David checks his watch, pulls out his cellphone, and dials a
number.

                         DAVID
                    Come on, Natalie.

INTERCUT - INT. NEWSROOM - NATALIE'S CUBICLE/SUBWAY STATION

Natalie is at her desk when the phone rings.

                         NATALIE
                    Metro.

                         DAVID
                    Natalie, thank God, it's me.

                         NATALIE
                    Where are you?

                         DAVID
                    In hell, that's where.

                         NATALIE
                    Huh?

                    DAVID
          Basically, I'm in the subway in
          Queens.

                    NATALIE
          Queens? How'd you manage that?

She starts laughing.

                    DAVID
          It's a long story. And it's not
          funny. Can you come and get me?

                    NATALIE
          Get you? What do you mean?

                    DAVID
          I'm stuck without any cash or
          tokens.

                    NATALIE
          Hit a money machine.

                    DAVID
          Believe me, I've tried.

                    NATALIE
          David, I can't just leave here.
          You're going to have to get here
          yourself.
               (beat)
          Take a cab. They take Visa. You
          brought your card, didn't you?

                    DAVID
          Brought it, yes, but...

                    NATALIE
          Listen, I gotta go. The managing
          editor wants to see me. I'll call
          you back.

David, left standing there, is not sure what to do.

Seeing a men's restroom nearby.

He enters it.

INT. MEN'S WASHROOM - CONTINUOUS

This restroom is where germs come to party.

David assess the damage of the morning in the scratched
mirror. Not too bad, but not perfect as before.

David straightens his tie. Hand combs his hair. Then washes his hands and face.

There are no paper towels to dry them with. He shakes his hands to dry them as best he can. His face still dripping.

Inside one of the stalls is toilet paper dispenser.

David enters, only to find the last person forgot to flush and apparently had spicy curry recently.

>   DAVID
>   Oh my...! That's inhuman!

While covering his nose, David reaches down to grab some toilet paper.

There is none.

Frustration is getting the better of David.

There is a SHUFFLING of feet in the next stall.

>   DAVID
>   Excuse me?
>   (beat)
>   Sorry to bother you. Could you
>   spare a few sheet of paper please?

Silence. Then the door latch CLICKS open.

>   DAVID
>   Hello?

A MALE VOICE responds.

>   MALE VOICE (O.C.)
>   Come on in. There's plenty.

Confusion.

>   DAVID
>   No thanks. Can you just pass some
>   under?

>   MALE VOICE
>   You want my paper, you have to come
>   get it yourself.

Realization.

David runs from the restroom.

INT. SUBWAY STATION

David checks his watch again.

As he prepares to leave, David notices a service door partly open.

He walks over to it, peers in, then pushes it open.

He then enters the tunnel.

INT. SERVICE TUNNEL

David is crawling through a tight service tunnel. As he crawls his foot gets caught on something and he is stuck.

> DAVID
> Oh, come on. What now?

David yanks his foot, but nothing gives.

> DAVID
> I can see the headline now: Man
> Found Dead Crawling Through Service
> Tunnel, Only Feet Keep Him From
> Salvation. That's not bad. Maybe I
> should give that one to Natalie
> just in case.

David continues to tug and tug with all his might.

Finally, his foot is freed and with it a huge cable is torn in half.

EXT. NEW YORK CITY SKYLINE

Several buildings' power goes out. A WOMAN SCREAMS. A MAN YELLS.

> WOMAN YELLING
> Dr. Phil? What happened to Dr.
> Phil?

INT. SERVICE TUNNEL

David holds up the cable, looks at it quizzically, then drops it.

> DAVID
> Hope that wasn't important.

David continues to crawl on through the tunnel, until he reaches an opening onto the tracks where he can stand and walk.

INT. SUBWAY TUNNEL

David looks down at his suit, which is now completely filthy and the knees are worn.

>   DAVID
>   Great, just fantastic!

A stone rolls between David's feet.

David sees another LOST MAN in a dirty business suit, looking lost and dejected walking the other way. They both stare at each other without saying a word as they pass.

INT. SUBWAY TUNNEL - LATER

David is still walking.

He stops and sniffs the air. There is a pungent odor.

He sniffs his armpits to see if it is him. It's not.

Slowly, David follows his nose to locate the origin of the foul stench.

Along the side of the tracks, there is a round vent with a slight green steam emitting from it.

As David gets closer he cringes at the smell.

>   DAVID
>   What the heck?

David peeks through the vents and sees a stream of raw sewage.

David turns away from the sight but leans against the vent.

>   DAVID
>   Either it's the East River, or its
>   a river of...

There is a CREAK.

David's eyes go wide and the vent falls in. David falls in with it.

SPLASH as David lands into the stream of refuse.

>   DAVID
>   ...Sh -- !

A subway train passes. THE NOISE OF THE TRAIN PASSING obscures David's scream.

INT. SEWER SYSTEM

David is on his hands and knees. He pulls what could be a
turd out of his shirt pocket and throws it away disgustedly.

>   DAVID
>   Ewww!

Frantically, David leaps about trying to get away from the
sewage, which completely surrounds him.

It is slippery and difficult for David to keep his footing.
He slips into the waste again.

>   DAVID
>   Ahh! Ahh!

David is hopping about crazily when he looks up and sees the
hole he made in the subway wall. He realizes that it is his
only escape from this river of putridity.

David plants his feet firmly and attempts to jump up.

He just barely misses the edge of the hole and falls back
down into the waste.

David stands and leaps for the hole again.

He grabs the lower edge and dangles helplessly.

Just then, he sees the head of an alligator swimming toward
him.

>   DAVID
>   Mommy!

He hangs there holding his breath.

The alligator notices him and snaps at his feet.

Pulling his knees up, David is just out of range.

The beast keeps moving.

David sighs relief.

>   DAVID
>   So the rumors are true.

David wiggles to pull himself up and out of the sewer. He
gets about halfway out of the tunnel and it looks like he is
going to make it, when a subway train comes speeding past.

The shock and force of the train passing cause David to lose his grip and fall back into the sewage.

INT. SERVICE TUNNEL

A New York City service crew is working on the electrical line that David tripped over and broke earlier.

There are two SERVICE MEN working on fixing the problem.

One has a tablet that is tuned into the local news where a report about the Mole-Man is being broadcast.

                    NEWSCASTER
          More news has surfaced regarding
          New York City's Mole-Man. Con
          Edison is blaming the Mole-Man for
          the recent power outage on the far
          east side of midtown. Nearly a half-
          dozen buildings are without power.
          Officials are unclear as to why the
          Mole-Man would attack the power
          supply for the city, but police
          believe this is just part of the
          escalation in the Mole-Man's hatred
          toward modern society. Police fear
          that the Mole-Man may be becoming
          increasingly violent to society at
          large and warn subway passengers to
          stay away from the Mole-Man if he
          is sighted and to also report him
          to local authorities.

On "...increasingly violent..." David passes by in the far distance, KICKING and SCREAMING and ACTING COMPLETELY MAD (MOS). The two service men do not notice him.

                    SERVICE GUY 1
          Hey, Benny did you hear that? They
          say this break in the line was
          caused by the Mole-Man. Go figure,
          ey.

INT. SUBWAY TUNNEL

David is SQUASHING along at a rapid pace.

                    DAVID
          I cannot believe my luck today.
          This is unbelievable.

David stops and looks around for some sign or demarcation of where he is.

                    DAVID
          Don't they have signs down here?
               (beat)
          No, of course not David. They don't
          expect people to get off the train
          and get themselves lost. Only an
          idiot would do such a thing.

David leans against the wall to rest. He doesn't realize he
is leaning against a steel door.

A bare light bulb flickers above his head as if he has had an
idea.

Now, he realizes he is leaning against a door. He tries the
handle but the door is locked.

                    DAVID
          Who would lock a door down here?

He shakes the handle and the knob plops off in his hand.

David looks about guiltily -- as if someone might be
watching.

He tosses the handle over his shoulder into the darkness.

With a swift kick the door busts open.

                    DAVID
          Right. Now we're getting somewhere.

David steps into a room.

INT. NEWSROOM - CONFERENCE ROOM - DAY

Natalie and other writers are sitting around a large table.
At the head is the MANAGING EDITOR.

                    MANAGING EDITOR
          How do we not have any additional
          information about who this Mole-man
          really is?

                    WRITER 1
          The police don't even know who he
          is boss.

                    MANAGING EDITOR
          We should know more than the
          police. We should always know more
          than the police. We are the news.

                    NATALIE
          I've been tracking a hunch that he
          worked in finances until the crash.
          I think that is why he is angry and
          dropped out.

                    MANAGING EDITOR
          Good. I like than angle. Pissed off
          one percenter strikes back against
          the very system that made, then
          broke him. Go with that.

                    NATALIE
          I have a few leads on employees of
          the various firms that had huge lay-
          offs. I could use some help
          tracking each down.

                    MANAGING EDITOR
          You got it. Volunteers?

Hands go up.

                    MANAGING EDITOR
          Great. See Natalie after. I like
          this. Tie it in with the Occupy
          Wall Street movement. Maybe the
          Mole-Man is embittered for being
          fired. Lost everything. Has to live
          underground. Love it. Do it.

INT. SERVICE ROOM

David has stepped into a small dark room. He uses his cell
phone to illuminate the room.

A single bare bulb hangs from the ceiling. David pulls the
string to turn it on.

Posters of swimsuit pin-ups are tacked to nearly every
surface. It's as if the office of *Sports Illustrated* exploded
all over the walls.

                    DAVID
          Where is here exactly?

A stack of porno magazines and three-ring binders rest on a
makeshift bookshelf.

David peeks inside the top magazine, acting like a teenage
boy in a convenience store worried that he will get caught.

               DAVID
         Wonder how long these have been
         here?

A NOISE out in the tunnel makes David jump and close the
magazine.

He stands still. Listening.

               DAVID
         What are you worried about, David?

He shakes it off.

               DAVID
         There's no one down here but you
         and some rats.

               ROBBER
         And don't forget us.

David spins around to see the three bank robbers blocking the
entrance to the room.

David is startled but quickly gains his wits.

               DAVID
         Hi there. This your place?

The gang step into the room fanning out around David. The one
who spoke is the obvious leader; he stands in front of David.

               DAVID
         I like what you've done with it.
         Nice collection of magazines too. I
         was just admiring . . .

               ROBBER
         Shut up!

               DAVID
         Right.

               ROBBER
         What do you want here?
            (beat)
         And what is that stench?

               DAVID
         Well, it's a long story -- one I'm
         sure you don't want to be bored
         with. So, I guess I'll be on my
         way.

                    ROBBER
          Not so fast, Sparky.

                    DAVID
          I needed to get City Hall so I
          caught the downtown express, but it
          broke down -- you know how they do
          that. I tried to catch another, but
          I got on one going the wrong way.
          Then I got off but I couldn't
          switch to the downtown side without
          paying again.

The robbers, increasingly annoyed, start looking at one
another like David is crazy. But he keeps ranting.

                    DAVID
          And I didn't have any money so I
          had to get cash. Well, let's just
          say that proved fruitless. So I
          decided to walk. Then I fell in the
          sewer. Yada, yada, yada and here I
          am. The door was open so I peeked
          in. Sorry, I didn't know this place
          belonged to anyone. Well, guess
          I'll be going now. Nice chatting.

One of the gang members pulls a butterfly knife and twirls
it.

David stops in his tracks.

The leader puts his face right into David's.

                    ROBBER
          It's not that easy.

                    DAVID
          I going to miss my interview.

                    ROBBER
          You're not getting no job smellin'
          like that.

                    DAVID
          Well, see, I have to catch a shower
          too then.

                    ROBBER
          Fine. You can go.

                    DAVID
          Great.

                        ROBBER
              As soon as you give us all your
              valuables.

                        DAVID
              Listen, I've already been robbed
              once today. I'm afraid you're too
              late.

                        ROBBER
              I thought you looked familiar.

The leader of the gang punches David in the face.

                        DAVID
              What was that for?

                        ROBBER
              For being a smart guy.

                        ROBBER
              Hand over the watch.

                        DAVID
              This? It's worthless, but here.
              It's yours.

David hands it to him.

                        ROBBER 2
              And the shoes.

                        DAVID
              Shoes? You're kidding.

The men take a step closer.

                        DAVID
              Okay, okay. Here.

He takes off his shoes and hands them over.

                        ROBBER
              What else you got?

                        DAVID
              That's all. Sorry.

                        ROBBER 2
              You wouldn't lie to us, would you?

                        DAVID
              Of course not. Why would I. It's
              like we are old friends.
                        (MORE)

                    DAVID (CONT'D)
          (beat)
     Pat me down if you want.

The robbers look at one another, as if to say "who wants to
touch the guy who smells like crap?"

David takes the opportunity to move toward the door.

Just then, his cellphone RINGS.

David stops.

                    DAVID
     Did you guys hear that? My ears are
     ringing so loud. Must be the
     trains.

The gang approach.

                    ROBBER
     You mother...I'm going to kill you.

David pulls out his phone.

                    DAVID
     Oh this? Here.

David tosses it to the leader, then takes off running.

Just then a subway train comes ROARING past. This stirs up
quite a wind in the room, throwing the magazines in the air
and sending the posters flapping.

In the confusion, David is able to exit the room into the
service tunnel, not caring which way he is going.

INT. SERVICE TUNNEL

The robbers are following and David blindly runs as fast as
he can. He makes it to a subway tunnel just in time.

INT. SUBWAY TUNNEL

Just in time to nearly be hit by a subway train.

David jumps to the side of the tunnel and is narrowly missed
by the train.

After it passes David jumps onto the tracks.

                    DAVID
     Okay, which one is the third rail?
          (beat)
     One.
                    (MORE)

>   DAVID (CONT'D)
>   (beat)
>   Two.
>   (beat)
>   Three. Great. Avoid that one.

He starts to move forward, then stops quickly.

>   DAVID
>   Or is it the second rail that's
>   juiced?

He checks behind him to see if the robbers are following.

A loud ZAPPING causes him to turn around to see a rat
exploding on the third rail.

>   DAVID
>   No, it's the third.

He crosses to the other side of the tracks.

The robbers are on the opposite side as another train passes
by.

David runs alongside the train as fast as he can to put as
much ground between him and the gang.

He finally comes across a Y in the tunnel. One way is
obviously the way the tunnel continues. The other way looks
to be an entrance to a different service tunnel.

Thinking he can fool the robbers, he enters the service
tunnel.

David eludes the gang but is left wandering through the
subway tunnels again.

>   DAVID
>   Great. Now what? I'm in New York
>   one week and I'm lost underground,
>   which -- little did I know -- was
>   more congested than a Tuesday in
>   midtown.

He walks along.

>   DAVID
>   No phone. No money. Only you,
>   David.

INT. NEWSROOM - CUBICLES - DAY

Natalie is conducting research on her computer. A fellow
WRITER, one of the volunteers approaches.

                         WRITER 2
            Did you hear about the bank
            robbery?

                         NATALIE
            No. Kind of focused today.

                         WRITER 2
            I wouldn't have mentioned it, but
            the robbers escaped into the subway
            around the same area that the black-
            out occurred. You think it's
            possible the Mole-Man has
            accomplices?

                         NATALIE
            That would be new news. He has
            never been seen with anyone before.

                         WRITER 2
            Just thought I would put it out
            there. Seems like a interesting
            coincidence.

The writer leaves Natalie to her research, but has her
thinking.

INT. SUBWAY SERVICE TUNNEL

David is walking along. He starts singing The Brady Bunch's
"Sunshine Day." This lightens his mood a bit.

He starts skipping his way down the tunnel.

There is some COMMOTION up ahead, the sound of something
FALLING TO THE GROUND.

David proceeds cautiously.

In front of him, he sees the back of an ARTIST painting on a
subway wall.

The artist, a member of the Bob Ross cult, has drawn a
rendition of the New York City skyline, with flames
overtaking it from below ground. The painting is very crude,
almost laughable.

The artist is mixing paint on his palette.

                         ARTIST
            Some phalo green, midnight black.
            That's nice. A touch of white.

He moves the brush up to his concrete canvas.

                    ARTIST
          Need a happy flame. There we go
          little friend. And a little
          companion here. A touch there... Oh
          gosh.
                (angrily)
          Not again. Man, I'll never get this
          right.

The artist's sudden change in temperament startles David and
he lets out a quiet GASP.

The artist turns and spots David watching.

                    ARTIST
          Who are you?

                    DAVID
          Sorry, I didn't mean to interrupt.

                    ARTIST
          This spot is taken. And don't even
          think of painting over "Dawn in
          Central Park" up ahead. That's my
          piece.

                    DAVID
          Oh, don't worry. I'm not an artist.

                    ARTIST
          That's for sure. Punk.

                    DAVID
          I'll be going.

                    ARTIST
          Fine.

The artist continues working with the paint.

                    ARTIST
          Some soft red, a touch of early
          dawn yellow.

David begins to walk away but stops and watches momentarily.

The artist moves the paint up to the wall again.

                    ARTIST
          Darn it. I'll never get this color
          right.

                  DAVID
You know, if I may interrupt, if
you want a soft shadow on the
Chrysler Building there you've got
to use a knife.

                  ARTIST
Knife?

                  DAVID
Yeah, you'll never get the right
effect with a brush.

                  ARTIST
I got some cans.

                  DAVID
No, no. Cans are for subway cars.
Is this graffiti or art?

                  ARTIST
Art.

                  DAVID
Well then, hand me a half-inch
knife.

The artist, obviously confused, looks at his supplies.

David, noticing that the artist has only brushes, reaches
down and picks up a rock.

                  DAVID
Here, let me show you.

David picks up some paint with the edge of his rock, makes a
series of frantic strokes, and succeeds in putting a shadow
on the Chrysler Building.

                  DAVID
There, you see.

                  ARTIST
That's nice. But then the fire
would shine off the boat pond too.

                  DAVID
Not a problem. You just take your
one-inch brush.

David picks it up.

                    DAVID
          Wash it, shake it. Then, mix up
          some magic orange, fire red, navy
          blue. Use the tips only. Lay down
          some soft color on shore here.

David does it. In the process accidently getting some paint
on his shirt.

                    ARTIST
          That's nice.

                    DAVID
          Then take your four-inch. It has to
          be dry. And soften the color by
          pulling it in one direction over
          the pond. Blend it in and viola.

                    ARTIST
          Incredible. You make it look easy.

                    DAVID
          Well, I'm no Degas.

                    ARTIST
          I'm not Italian either.

                    DAVID
          The key is to feel the canvas, feel
          the color. It would help to have
          some more light down here.

                    ARTIST
          Yeah, it's not easy. That's why I
          like it. Anybody can paint on
          canvas. Only a select few can paint
          here.
               (beat)
          Teach me something else.

                    DAVID
          Teach you? Well, I don't think I'm
          qualified.

                    ARTIST
          Come on, really. You're good, man.
          Show me how to paint a stream or a
          mountain.

                    DAVID
          Really, I'd like to. But I can't do
          that stuff. I'm just a hack with a
          brush.

                              DAVID
            Also, I'm late for an appointment.
            I've got to get going.

                              ARTIST
            Stick around man.

                              DAVID
            I can't.

                              ARTIST
            Come on. I'll do your portrait.

                              DAVID
            Nah.

                              ARTIST
             You can paint my portrait.

David shakes his head no and walks away.

The artist follows.

David picks up the pace to get away. Suddenly this has turned
awkward. Creepy.

The artist follows.

David is running now.

The artist is running too.

                              ARTIST
            Come on, man. I'll pose nude.

                              DAVID
             No thanks.

INT. SUBWAY TUNNEL - LATER

David rounds a corner and it is quiet and dark again.

He walks along until he finds some stairs. What the hell?

At the bottom is a rusting metal door. David opens the door
pokes his head through and is taken aback --

INT. UNDERGROUND ROOM

A ladder leads from the door down to the equivalent of an
apartment. All the conveniences of a normal home just dirtier
and a mile underground.

After considering it for a moment, David climbs down and explores the apartment.

A bottle whizzes by his ear and shatters against one of the walls.

David turns quickly and can see two eyes staring at him from out of the darkness. A man, PAPA, speaks.

                    PAPA
          Who are you?

                    DAVID
          No one, I mean...

                    PAPA
          What are you doing here?

                    DAVID
          Actually, oh my God. This isn't my
          apartment after all. It looks just
          like it. I've got that very same...

David looks around and spots a dirty cup sitting near the sink.

                    DAVID
          ...coffee cup.
               (beat)
          But, sure enough, this isn't my
          place. I'll just be going. Which
          way to 92nd and Lex?

                    PAPA
          You're a cop.

                    DAVID
          No, no cop. Just passing through.
          I'll be going.

                    PAPA
          No you won't.

Papa steps out of the darkness.

As he does, David turns the other way. But from that corridor a second set of eyes comes closer.

Papa (late 40s) is a proud homeless man. He has a thick, dirty beard and ripped clothes. He carries a cane.

The second person, BULLET (30), is the type of homeless person you avoid at all costs. His thick dreadlocks drape over bare arms that are as thick as most people's legs.

Bullet stands in David's way with his arms crossed.

>   PAPA
>   I'm afraid we can't let you leave.

>   BULLET
>   No one leaves.

Bullet hisses.

Papa is now a few feet in front of David.

David notices a few other people behind Papa in tunnel, including a woman, MANDY, and a child, JESSICA. All are watching David.

>   PAPA
>   You're on our turf now. This is our
>   home. Home of the Chuds.
>   (beat)
>   Ever hear of the Chuds?

>   DAVID
>   (more nervous)
>   No, but I'm sure you're a nice gang
>   ...group.

Bullet gets in David's face.

>   BULLET
>   Chuds -- cannibalistic human
>   underground dwellers.

>   DAVID
>   You didn't happen to say
>   'drillers'?

>   BULLET
>   And we're hungry.

Time to panic.

David looks around nervously for an escape.

The men's icy stares continue.

David takes off running toward the ladder. When he reaches it, the entire group of people starts laughing.

David stops and looks back.

They are all whooping it up. Those in the tunnel turn away laughing. Then Papa lets him off the hook.

                    PAPA
          It's okay, son.

He meets David at the ladder and tries to help him down with
a reassuring hand.

                    PAPA
          We're just messing with you. It's
          not too often that some young
          socialite visits.
                    (beat)
          Have a seat.
                    (to the woman)
          Get him some coffee, will you?

David is even more shocked now.

Both men pull up a chair; Bullet just stares at David with a
demented look.

Jessica stands at the table.

                    PAPA
          You okay?

                    DAVID
          I guess. What was that Chud stuff
          about?

                    PAPA
          Don't worry, son. Keeps the riff
          raff out. I'm sure you've heard
          stories about how we eat anyone who
          comes down here.

                    DAVID
          Actually, no. I just moved here.

                    BULLET
          Just moved here, and you show up
          seven stories under the city.
                    (to Papa)
          I find that...kind of funny.

                    PAPA
          Settle down, Bullet.

David looks alarmed.

                    DAVID
          Bullet?

                    PAPA
          Where are my social graces? I'm
          Papa. That's Mandy and this is
          little Jessica.

Jessica sticks her tongue out at David and turns away.

A HUMMING comes from the kitchen. David looks puzzled.

                    PAPA
          Microwave.

                    DAVID
          Microwave?

                    PAPA
          Yeah. You drink your coffee hot,
          right?

                    DAVID
          Yes.

The microwave DINGS.

Mandy takes a cup out.

                    MANDY
          Cream and sugar?

                    DAVID
          Black is perfect.

                    BULLET
          You better believe it is.

Mandy puts the cup down in front of David.

                    DAVID
          Thanks.

                    PAPA
          Welcome to our home.

                    DAVID
          You all live here?

                    MAN
          Yep, this is our family.

                    DAVID
          How many are there?

                    PAPA
          In our community about 50. But
          there are many others underground.

                    DAVID
          Communities?

                    PAPA
          Yep, dozens of them. Some more
          organized than others. Some have
          elected mayors, others just rob
          from one another.

                    DAVID
          Wow.

                    PAPA
          I don't know how many people.
          Getting a bit crowded for my taste.
               (beat)
          Between you and me, not all of them
          are as nice as we are.

David glances at Bullet.

                    DAVID
          Oh, really?

                    PAPA
          Don't worry about Bullet. He's
          harmless. A bit eccentric, maybe.
          Most of us mole-men are...how
          should I put it...three bricks shy
          of three bricks.

                    DAVID
          Mole-men? There's more than one of
          you?

Papa laughs.

                    PAPA
          We're all mole-men, son, although I
          never much cared for the term.

                    DAVID
          I mean the one the police are
          chasing.

                    PAPA
          The police are chasing all of us.
          It's Dragon today, me tomorrow,
          Bullet the next day.

                    DAVID
Dragon?

                    PAPA
Yeah, lives under Penn Station. A
nice guy really, just got into some
trouble and went underground.

                    DAVID
What sort of trouble?

                    PAPA
The same trouble we all get in.
Drugs, robbery...

                    BULLET
Murder.

                    PAPA
Put a lid on it Bull.
     (to David)
He's not used to visitors.

                    DAVID
I see.

                    PAPA
Dragon's a good guy, but Bullet is
right. Dragon killed a guy years
ago and some people in Times Square
witnessed it. What they didn't see
was Dragon saving a woman's life.
Some crack-head was busting her
over the head with a pipe 'n
probably wanted her to turn tricks
for him. Dragon saved her.

                    DAVID
That's why they're chasing him?

                    PAPA
Ah, you know how these stories go.
Every culture needs its myth and
the Mole-Man is one of ours. Every
time someone is hit by a train or
robbed on a platform, Dragon gets
blamed. It just fuels the legend.
In reality, he's harmless. A real
pranskter though. I think he enjoys
being seen once in a while just to
shake things up.

                          DAVID
                So, do you all know one another? I
                mean all the homeless.

Papa's demeanor changes.

                          PAPA
                We're houseless, not homeless.

                          DAVID
                Oh, sorry.

                          PAPA
                Homeless implies you belong
                nowhere, you have no community, no
                family. We have that. We just don't
                have houses.

                          DAVID
                I apologize.

                          PAPA
                And no, we don't all know one
                another. But after you've been here
                a few years, you recognize faces.

                          DAVID
                A few years. How long have you been
                down here?

                          PAPA
                Almost ten years. But I've been
                lucky. Most don't live that long...
                they die after a few years from
                drugs, AIDS, or just plain
                loneliness.

                          DAVID
                How have you survived?

                          PAPA
                It's been quite easy really. It's
                warm, much warmer than on the
                street. And we get water from the
                leaking pipes down a ways.

He points.

                          PAPA
                We have light. Pick a wire and just
                tap it for electricity. The best
                part is no bill every month.

David looks up and sees a bunch of wires.

                    DAVID
          What about food?

                    PAPA
          Food? Hell, you don't starve in New
          York. Too much food is thrown away.
          And even when we do get hungry,
          there's always the track rabbits.

                    DAVID
          Track rabbits?

                    PAPA
          Rats. Huge. Juicy. Meaty.

                    DAVID
          You eat the rats?

                    PAPA
          Sure. We eat them.
              (beat)
          Before they eat us.

Just then, there's a COMMOTION in the corridor.

A young man comes into the room, then stops when he sees
David.

                    PAPA
          It's okay. He's a friend.

The man grunts.

                    DAVID
          I should be going.

David stands up.

Papa puts his hand on his shoulder and pushes him into his
seat.

                    PAPA
          Son, do me one favor when you go
          upstairs?

David nods.

                    PAPA
          Tell them to quit trying to save
          us.

                    DAVID
          Who?

                         PAPA
          They sweep these tunnels every
          week. We have to turn off our
          lights and hide.
                    (beat)
          I've been thrown out of Penn
          Station, Grand Central, the
          Rotunda, Thompkins Square. Every
          time, I was sent to Bellvue or Fort
          Washington, only to be robbed and
          beaten and back on the street and
          back underground. It's safer here.
          It's our home. We want to stay
          here.

                         DAVID
          But there's a whole world up there.

                         PAPA
          A whole world that doesn't need or
          want us. And we don't want it.
          We're the refuge of society. The by-
          product of a world that's gone
          wrong. Most people down here have a
          drug problem. The rest a mental
          problem. The world up there threw
          us out so we had to find our own
          world. Our whole world is down here
          now, son.

                         DAVID
          You don't want help?

                         BULLET
          We don't need no help.

                         DAVID
          Huh?

                         PAPA
          Most of us couldn't make it
          topside. I know I couldn't. I'm
          nobody up there. I'm Papa here.
          People look up to me, think I'm
          wise. I'm like Moses down here and
          these are my people.

                         DAVID
          What about your family?

                         PAPA
          This is my family.

                    DAVID
          I mean your real family.

                    PAPA
          This is my real family.
               (beat)
          As far as any blood relatives, they
          don't exist anymore. Haven't since
          I ran away when I was 11.

                    DAVID
          You're a runaway?

                    PAPA
          Hell yeah. My father was a bastard.

                    DAVID
          Where'd you go?

                    PAPA
          Where didn't I go. I went from
          being homeless to foster care, from
          homeless to jail, from homeless to
          underground.
               (beat)
          Believe me, I tried to go straight.
          Didn't work. Got mixed up dealing
          drugs, taking drugs. I tried
          welfare, food stamps, shelters,
          detox. I've been through it all.
          Now I'm here. And I'm at peace.
               (beat)
          Once you're down here, you can't go
          back up. We live out our lives
          here, with our families, and then
          we die. End of story.

                    DAVID
          There must be some people who would
          rather live normal lives.

                    PAPA
          I suppose. Not me.

David is quiet. He looks over to Jessica, who is now playing
with a beat-up doll.

                    DAVID
          What about her?

                    PAPA
          What about her?

                    DAVID
          You don't think she can be helped?

Papa shrugs.

                    PAPA
          I don't know. Maybe.

                    DAVID
          She still has a chance.

                    PAPA
          She doesn't need a chance. She
          needs a home. She has that, or at
          least some semblance of it, here.

                    DAVID
          She's a baby.

                    PAPA
          She's six. Down here, that's a
          young woman.

                    DAVID
          Up there, she'd have a family that
          could provide for her. Send her to
          college.

                    PAPA
          College? What good's that? I know
          people underground with degrees.

                    DAVID
          Yeah?

                    PAPA
          Yeah! Didn't help them any. They
          lived in that world and came down
          here.

David shakes his head. Difficult to fathom.

                    DAVID
          It'd be a shame if she never had
          the opportunity to try.

Papa sits quietly.

                    DAVID
          Well, I'd better get going. Thanks
          for the talk.

He walks to the ladder and climbs it. Papa calls out.

> > PAPA
> > Son.
> > (beat)
> > You never saw us.

David nods.

Papa motions to Jessica playing on the floor.

> > PAPA
> > But, if you want, you can tell them
> > about her.

David nods again and climbs out of the apartment.

INT. SUBWAY TUNNEL

David walks through the tunnel.

> > DAVID
> > Unbelievable. There truly is
> > another world down here.

The walls are covered with graffiti. David comes upon a sign
that reads "Heaven." It points to the right.

Curious, David goes that way.

As he keeps walking, David passes a few more "Heaven" signs.

Finally David reaches a rusty door with the words "No, silly,
it's Iowa" scrawled above it.

David peeks inside the door.

INT. UNDERGROUND CHAMBER

What he sees absolutely astonishes him.

At least a dozen people are playing softball around a small
baseball diamond.

David closes the door and walks away.

> > DAVID
> > Too weird.

INT. NEWSROOM - NATALIE'S CUBICLE - DAY

Natalie dials her phone. She waits for the phone to connect.

When it connects she begins talking.

                    NATALIE
          David, hi. Listen, I'm not going to
          be able to make it to lunch this
          afternoon. There is just too much
          going on around here. The Mole-Man
          has been causing quite a commotion
          and we're trying to stay on top of
          it. I hope you unders--

                    ROBBER
          Lady, take a breath.

                    NATALIE
          David?

INTERCUT NATALIE'S CUBICLE/ INT. SUBWAY

                    ROBBER
          Yeah.

                    NATALIE
          This isn't David. Who is this?

                    ROBBER
          Who is this?

                    NATALIE
          Where's David?

                    ROBBER
          He can't make it to the phone right
          now. He'll call you back.

                    NATALIE
          What do you mean?

                    ROBBER
          He's...ah...in the shower.

                    NATALIE
          In the shower? He's still at the
          apartment?

                    ROBBER
          No, the club.

                    NATALIE
          Huh? What club?

                    ROBBER
          Yeah, he said you might call and to
          tell you that he and Linda are
          busy.

                        NATALIE
           Linda? Who's she?

                        ROBBER
           Hey, what do I know? He told me to
           hold his phone for him.

                        NATALIE
           He's going to be holding his head
           when I get through with him.
           Listen, give him a message.

                        ROBBER
           Sure.
                (sarcastically)
           Let me grab a pen.

                        NATALIE
           Ready?

                        ROBBER
           Start talking.

                        NATALIE
           Tell hm I can't make it to lunch
           and to call Natalie immediately.
           Also, tell him that Linda better be
           his imaginary friend or he's a dead
           man.
                (beat)
           Got it.

                        ROBBER
           Every word.

                        NATALIE
           Read it back.

INT. SUBWAY

The thug gives the phone a dirty look and throws it into the
darkness of the subway tunnel.

Natalie's VOICE is still railing on.

                        ROBBER
           Man, I feel sorry for that Donald
           dude.

As the gang of thugs walk away, a shadowy figure reaches from
the darkness and picks up the phone.

INT. SUBWAY TUNNEL

David is walking when he steps into a large puddle of water
with his socked foot.

David slowly lifts his foot out of the water puddle and lets
the water drip off him.

> DAVID
> Lovely, just lovely.

David notices a grate to the street above on the other side
of the tracks.

He crosses the downtown and uptown tracks -- carefully
avoiding the third rail.

He tries to reach the grate. A bar parallel to the ground is
situated near the grate. He reaches for that, but it is too
high.

David jumps from the edge of a ledge and reaches for the bar.

He misses and falls into more putrid standing water on the
track.

A TRAIN IS COMING.

David quickly gets up and climbs on top of the uptown
walkway.

David jumps onto and across the uptown track and attempts to
climb the supports between the uptown and downtown tracks.

He reaches for the bar. Success!

Once there, he is able to push the grate open and climb out
of the tunnel.

EXT. CITY STREET--DAY

Above ground, David takes stock in his appearance via a
reflection in a large window. His suit is wet, muddy, and
ripped. His face dirty and swollen, a nice black eye. His
hair's a mess. No shoes.

David is standing right in front of a very fancy restaurant.

The MAITRE'D, standing at the door, gives David a dirty look.

David looks at the menu through the window and
realizes...this is Billy's! <u>The restaurant in which he is
supposed to meet Natalie.</u>

                    DAIVD
          Well, I guess that's one way to get
          here.

David checks his watch only to realize it is not there.

He shrugs and walks toward the door.

The Maitre'd notices David coming and prepares for the
confrontation.

As David tries to enter the Maitre'd stops him by putting up
his hand.

                    MAITRE'D
          I don't think so, sir.

                    DAVID
          I'm meeting my girlfriend.

                    MAITRE'D
          Here?

                    DAVID
          Yes.

                    MAITRE'D
          No.

                    DAVID
          She's probably waiting inside.

                    MAITRE'D
          Ah, yes, she arrived a few minutes
          ago. I believe she came out of that
          manhole over there.
               (pointing)

                    DAVID
          Oh, that. You see, I had...
          Nevermind. She probably came by
          cab.

                    MAITRE'D
          Trust me, sir, nobody is waiting
          inside for you.

                    DAVID
          Well, why don't you let me make
          sure?

                    MAITRE'D
          We have a dress code, sir.

                         DAVID
              Dress code?

                         MAITRE'D
              Jackets are required.

                         DAVID
              I'm wearing a jacket.

The Maitre'd looks him up and down.

                         MAITRE'D
              Is that Mizrahi's au de sewer line?

                         DAVID
              I fell into some water, that's
              all...

                         MAITRE'D
              Good day, sir.

                         DAVID
              No, you see, I was running through
              the subway tunnel and I fell...

The Maitre'd closes the door in David's face.

David turns as if he is going to walk away.

Then, he bursts passed the Maitre'd and races into the
restaurant.

INT. RESTUARANT

A few waiters quickly block his path.

                         DAVID
              Natalie? Natalie? Natalie?

The waiters grab him and drag him back out the door.

EXT. CITY STREET

David is unceremoniously tossed out of the restaurant.

David rolls onto the sidewalk and upends a MAN who just
ordered a hot dog from a street foodcart.

Hot dogs go flying. They land on David. A rain of mustard,
ketchup and relish follow.

The man jumps to his feet.

David, frustrated, is wiping the mustard off his face.

                    HOTDOG MAN
          What's your problem, buddy?

                    DAVID
               (pointing to the
               restaurant)
          They just tossed me out of there.

                    HOTDOG MAN
          You some sort of tough guy?

                    DAVID
          It wasn't my fault.

                    HOTDOG MAN
          You owe me for the dogs.

                    DAVID
          Interest? It wasn't my fault.

The man looks menacing.

                    DAVID
          Okay, okay. I'll buy a new hotdog.

He reaches in his suit, then remembers that he lost his
wallet.

                    DAVID
          I will...but right now I don't have
          any money.

The man balls up his fist.

                    DAVID
          But hey, I'll pay you back. I'll
          owe you.

David pulls picks a napkin from the foodcart.

                    DAVID
          Do you have a pen? I'll write an
          official IOU. All nice and legal.

The man slaps the napkin from his hand.

                    HOTDOG MAN
          You'll pay now. With your pretty-
          boy face.

                    DAVID
          Yeah?

                         HOTDOG MAN
          Yeah.

David puffs up like a tough guy too, then takes off running.

The man gives chase.

INT. SUBWAY STATION

David ducks down the stairs into the subway station to get
away from the man.

The man is close behind. Looking for David in the crowd.

David walks up to the turnstiles but spots a POLICE OFFICER
watching.

David is torn: Should he get beat up by crazed hot dog guy?
Or, should he risk being arrested by jumping the turnstile to
get away?

David hesitates too long. A crowd is bunching up behind him
and people are YELLING.

This draws attention. The police officer approaches David.

David watches the police officer and looks back at the hot
dog guy who appears to have given up looking for David and
exits the subway.

Crisis averted.

David smiles weakly at the police officer and steps away from
the turnstile.

David walks over against the wall to think. A small cup sits
at David's feet.

                         DAVID
               Think David, think.
                    (to a passerby)
               Excuse me sir, do you know what
               time it is?

                         TIME GUY
               Two o'clock. Here, get yourself
               cleaned up.

The man drops a quarter into the cup.

David looks up surprised and astonished.

                         DAVID
               Yeah, this will get me far.

> TIME GUY
> Ungrateful schmuck. Get a friggin'
> job, you ingrate.

> DAVID
> (angrily)
> Believe it or not, that's what I've
> been trying to do this entire day.

The passerby is intimidated and rushes away.

> DAVID
> That's the only thing New Yorkers
> seem to understand.

David picks out the quarter. He has an epiphany.

> DAVID
> (to self)
> Two o'clock. I can still get back
> to my apartment, change clothes,
> and make it on time to my meeting.

David throws the quarter in the air, smiling.

He picks up the cup.

> DAVID
> (calling out)
> Alms? Alms for the poor. Alms?

People walk past David giving him strange and disgusted
looks.

David smiles sheepishly, desperately trying to earn enough
for a subway ticket.

> DAVID
> (calling out)
> Alms? Alms for the poor. Alms?

No one pays any attention to him.

One LITTLE BOY being pulled along by his MOTHER kicks David
in the shin.

> DAVID
> Owww. You little snothole.

David reassesses the situation. He starts singing --
horribly.

A few people nearby scatter, a few others give him dirty
looks.

A businessman walks by.

                    BUSINESSMAN
          Give you a buck to shut up.

                    DAVID
          I'll take it.

                    BUSINESSMAN
          Screw you. Shut up anyway.

David is slightly offended and more frustrated.

                    DAVID
          Maybe I'm being too old-fashioned
          about this.

Another group of people pass David.

                    DAVID
          Hey man, spare some change. Give it
          up.

Again, no one looks at David except THE old couple.

David recognizes them from earlier in the day.

                    OLD WOMAN
          Look, there's that nice young boy.

                    OLD MAN
          Hey, it sure is. Let's apologize
          for what happened earlier.

                    OLD WOMAN
          Young man...

                    DAVID
          Oh no. Stay away from me.

                    OLD MAN
          It's okay son. We'd like to
          apologize.

                    OLD WOMAN
          We want to make it up to you.

                    DAVID
          Really? Well, could you loan me a
          couple bucks for a MetroCard?

                    OLD WOMAN
          Sure we could.

                    OLD MAN
          But we won't.

                    DAVID
          Huh?

                    OLD MAN
          You've got to take some pride in
          yourself. Pull yourself up by your
          bootstraps.

                    OLD WOMAN
          We don't believe in charity.

                    DAVID
          It's not charity. I'll pay you
          back.

                    OLD MAN
          We've heard that one before.

                    OLD WOMAN
          We sure have. We have a son about
          your age. He used to be a loser
          just like you.

                    DAVID
          I'm not a loser.

                    OLD MAN
          Now he's a successful broker. He
          lives uptown in a big two-bedroom
          on Seventy-nineth Street.

                    DAVID
          Listen, I could really use some
          help. Can't you just loan me a
          dollar? I mean, you sprayed me with
          mace earlier.

                    OLD WOMAN
          It was pepper spray.

                    OLD MAN
          Mace is illegal in New York.

                    DAVID
          Whatever. Come on. Just a buck.

David reaches for the woman's purse.

She screams and starts beating David with it.

David throws up his arms to deflect the blows to his face.

                    DAVID
        Stop it.

But the old woman doesn't stop. She just keeps whacking David
about the head and shoulders with her purse.

A few passersby take notice.

                    PASSERBY 1
        That guy tried to rob that nice old
        couple.

                    PASSERBY 2
        Let's get him.

A group starts moving toward David.

The woman pulls out her pepper spray. She blasts David again.

David SCREAMS in pain.

One of the passerby grabs the can from the woman and blasts
David again.

David SCREAMS again.

                    DAVID
        You old bats!

                    OLD MAN
        Kids today.

                    OLD WOMAN
        You just can't talk to them.

The couple and the passersby walk away.

David struggles to regain his composure.

A HOMELESS GUY walks up to David and stares at him.

                    DAVID
        Can I help you?

The little man says nothing, but continues to stare at David.

                    DAVID
        Go away. Shoo.

David tries to shoo the man away, but the man continues to
stand in front of David. David is exasperated.

                    DAVID
        What?

David looks down at his hand to the quarter there.

>   DAVID
>   Here, is this what you want? It's
>   the only money I have, go ahead
>   take it.

The man takes the quarter.

>   DAVID
>   You're welcome.

The man reaches into his filthy clothes and rummages around
in some deep pocket trying to find something.

>   DAVID
>   No that's quite all right, you keep
>   whatever you have there. I'm sure
>   you need it more than I do.

But the man keeps rummaging until he pulls David's cellular
phone out.

He places it in David's hand, turns, and walks away.

David looks down. Amazed to see his phone.

>   DAVID
>   My phone! Sweet hallelujah!

When David looks up, the homeless man has disappeared.

David presses the POWER button only to find the battery is
nearly drained.

>   DAVID
>   Of course.

David walks toward the turnstile that leads to the subway
when he spots the police officer watching him.

>   DAVID
>   That's not good.

A train pulls into the station.

>   DAVID
>   Must reach train.

The police officer is watching David intently.

David looks to see what the path is like to the turnstile and
then the subway ramp.

David looks again at the police officer.

He is still watching David.

David makes a break for it. IN SLOW MOTION David runs toward the turnstile, pushing past a few people as he runs.

The police officer, anticipating David's actions, runs to cut him off.

David is sprinting with all he is made of to reach the turnstile before the police officer.

As David nears the turnstile, the kid who kicked him in the shin walks in front of him. The kid smiles as if he somehow knows he is obstructing David's path.

David jumps up.

The police office leaps toward David to tackle him.

David places one foot on the kid's head to push off from.

The police officer tackles the kid.

David leaps over the turnstile and lands safely on the other side

The police office and the kid crumble into a tangle of legs and arms.

The mother SCREAMS.

David runs to catch the train.

INT. SUBWAY PLATFORM

David reaches the platform. It is too late.

The train doors have closed and it is about to pull away.

David races to catch the train, running the length of the platform as the train gains speed and leaves the station.

At the last possible moment he leaps and catches the handrails on the back of the last car.

INT. SUBWAY TUNNEL

David is hanging on for dear life.

He positions himself and looks into the car for some help.

Amazingly, it is Natalie who is sitting near the door.

                              DAVID
                    What are the odds of this?

David BANGS on the window to get Natalie's attention.

INT. SUBWAY CAR

Natalie is engrossed in the documents she is reading on her
tablet. The ear buds she is wearing BLAST music.

David's face is peaking in the window in the background as he
BANGS desperately to get her attention.

David finally quits BANGING. He is frustrated. So close.

He hangs wearily from the back of the car.

Natalie pulls out her cellular phone and dials.

EXT. SUBWAY CAR

David's phone RINGS.

David realizes that Natalie is calling him.

He reaches into his pocket for his phone.

Several times he almost slips off the train but is able to
hang on.

                              DAVID
                    Hold on Natalie. Hold on! Please
                    let the battery last long enough.

David finally gets the phone out of his pocket.

The phone keeps RINGING. Natalie is growing impatient in the
background.

He slides his nose across the screen to activate the call.

The phone call connects!

David is crying for joy.

INT. SUBWAY CAR

                              NATALIE
                    David? David, are you there?

We see David through the window as he moves the phone up to
his ear.

When the train hits a turn David slips and fumbles with the phone. As it spins in the air David almost catches it.

It falls.

In one last-ditch effort to catch it, David leaps for the phone.

David SCREAMS as he falls from the train.

> NATALIE
> David! This isn't funny. What are
> you doing? David?

INT. SUBWAY TUNNEL

The train disappears down the tunnel.

David's hand raises into the air with the cellular phone in it. He caught it!

As David tries to lift himself up, the phone slips from his hand and falls to the ground, bouncing once and touching the third rail.

The phone EXPLODES into a shower of sparks which David must shield himself from.

The phone is dead.

David stares at the burned puddle of phone in disbelief.

Finally he shrugs and starts walking.

David looks like an opponent of Mike Tyson after three rounds.

> DAVID
> There's got to be a better way to
> get around in this city.

MONTAGE

-- David walking alone.

-- Subway trains passing him as he walks.

-- David notices a figure walking toward him on the opposite side of the tracks. As the figure comes closer David realizes it is the same Lost Man that he passed earlier.

As they pass each other they nod a nod of recognition.

As before without a word, and as quick as he appears, the Lost Man is gone. David continues on.

INT. SUBWAY TUNNEL

David stops, puts his hand on his knees and breathes deeply.

He hears the soft THUMP OF MUSIC from somewhere up ahead.

>   DAVID
>   What the?

David jogs, which is difficult considering he is not wearing shoes.

The further he jogs LOUDER THE MUSIC.

Then it STOPS.

>   DAVID
>   Nooooo!

The MUSIC starts again. It is some sort of TECHNO MUSIC.

>   DAVID
>   Thank you.

David speed-walks until he comes to a small metal door from behind which the MUSIC seems to be coming.

David pushes on the door and it pops open.

INT. LARGE UNDERGROUND CHAMBER

David is backstage of an underground performance art theater.

On the make-shift stage, a woman wearing a purple spandex bodysuit is laying spread eagle on the ground. A man in a head-to-toe black leather outfit and a whip is stalking the woman.

Loudspeakers are pumping out the TECHNO MUSIC and a running dialog --

>   MAN IN BLACK
>   So Jezebel, I find you at last, you
>   slut. I shall strike you down and
>   give you the thirty-nine lashes
>   that you have brought upon yourself
>   for your indiscretion.

David stands completely still watching the scene unfold before his eyes. To say he is confused and perplexed would be an understatement.

                    MAN IN BLACK
          Thirty-nine. Thirty-nine. I shall
          whip you thirty-nine times.

                    WOMAN PERFORMER
          Whip me. Whip me. I want to feel
          the cold leather against my warm
          body.

                    MAN IN BLACK
          You slut. You harlot. You don't
          deserve my whipping.

                    DAVID
          These people are nuts.

Unbeknownst to David, he is standing near a microphone. His
voice is amplified into the entire chamber.

The crowd GASPS.

The people on-stage turn to look at David and a spotlight
from out of the darkness pans to him.

He stands there.

The entire room staring at him. The MUSIC has stopped.

The man in the black leather outfit charges David.

                    MAN IN BLACK
          Who is this infidel? One of your
          callers, I suppose. You wench. How
          many men will it take to satisfy
          your deep urges?

David is horrified.

                    DAVID
          Look, I am terribly sorry if I
          ruined your little rendezvous here.
          It seems awfully nice -- in a
          dirty, sewer system kind of way.

The woman in purple reaches David and wraps her arms and legs
around him caressing his hair and kissing his neck. She
leaves large purple lip marks on him every time she kisses
him.

                    WOMAN PERFORMER
          Yes, it is true, this is my lover.
          He is a hundred times more the man
          than you could ever be.

                    DAVID
          Not true, not true. I don't even
          know her. And since you all seem to
          be very busy doing something
          somewhat, ah, demented, please
          don't let me interrupt.

                    MAN IN BLACK
          Quiet! You both shall pay.

David is trying to disengage himself from the woman, but she
continues to tangle herself around him.

                    DAVID
          I'll just go out the way I came in.
          Thanks and sorry for the
          interruption.

                    MAN IN BLACK
          You will go nowhere, you dog of
          hell. It is time to repent!

The man in black grabs David by the back of the neck and
throws him to the ground. The woman tumbles on top of him.

                    DAVID
          Hey now...

                    MAN IN BLACK
          Quiet, you shall pay for your sin.

A huge blast of steam rises from the ground and colorful
lights descend from the ceiling.

The TECHNO MUSIC blasts again.

DANCERS leap onto the stage.

As a group they lift David and spin him.

When David is finally placed on his feet again, the dancers
and other performers retreat to backstage leaving David alone
before the audience.

From out of the darkness a over ripe tomato flies and SPLATS
against David. This is followed by more projectile fruit.

The lights are SPINNING frantically and the music is reaching
an EAR-BREAKING PITCH.

The girl in purple returns and as the music reaches a
crescendo, she throws a bucket of white paint all over David.

The music STOPS. The lights GO BLACK.

Out of the darkness the audience begins to applaud wildly.

The lights come back up and the man in black and the woman in purple take bow.

Next the dancers bow.

David stands, center stage, dripping wet with paint wondering...<u>what the hell is going on?!</u>

The other performers part and raise their hands to David as if presenting him to the audience.

The audience goes mad with applause.

David takes a bow. Then another.

The HOUSELIGHTS come ON and the audience wanders out.

The cast filter off the stage. No one seems to take any notice of David any longer.

The man in black walks up to David and shakes his hand.

>   MAN IN BLACK
>   Nice entrance. You Bobby G's boy?

>   DAVID
>   Bobby G?

>   MAN IN BLACK
>   Bobby G's the man. Tell him Ball
>   Bearing appreciates him sending you
>   over.

>   DAVID
>   Sure.

The man in black begins to walk away, then turns around.

>   MAN IN BLACK
>   Hey, don't be a stranger. You got
>   talent boy. You're going to make
>   it. Maybe even above-ground.

David shakes his head affirmatively.

Before long, David is left completely alone as if the entire event never took place.

A voice out of the darkness shouts out.

                    VOICE (O.C.)
          Lock up on your way out, will you
          buddy? Thanks.

                    DAVID
          But, but, where is out? Hello?
          Hello?

The last light is turned off and David finds himself alone in
the dark once again.

                    DAVID
          Hey! Anybody still here? Ahhhhh.

A CUTAWAY VERSION OF THE EARTH shows David standing in the
chamber several floors underground, above him is dirt, subway
tunnels, a subway station, more dirt and finally the world
above-ground.

INT. SUBWAY TUNNEL

David is back walking through the dark tunnels.

                    DAVID
          Maybe this is how people get stuck
          under New York. Maybe my bad day is
          someone else's drug problem or act
          of desperation. Maybe I should just
          resign myself to the fact that I'll
          never get out.

A rat scurries by.

David jumps back.

                    DAVID
          Forget that. I've got to get out of
          here.

He begins walking faster and faster.

                    DAVID
          There's got to be a way out.

After walking for a while a platform appears up ahead.

David walks out of the tunnel and onto the platform.

A few people give him a strange look. A few walk around him.
Most just ignore him.

David stops and looks at the sign. It's the Spring Street
station.

David stops a stranger.

>   DAVID
>   Trains stop here?

>   STRANGER
>   Every few minutes.

The stranger walks away.

David finds an empty seat.

>   DAVID
>   Sorry mayor, but I'm going home.
>   Hope we can meet some other time.

David slumps down in his seat. He is exhausted, but resists
the urge to fall asleep.

A train approaches.

David walks to the edge of the platform to board. He notices
the people give him dirty looks.

He moves farther down the platform and enters the train in
the last car.

INT. SUBWAY CAR

There are only a few other people in this car.

David finds a seat.

David leans his head back to rest.

At the next stop everyone exits.

The old couple from earlier get on.

David notices them immediately but hopes they won't see him.

They do.

>   OLD WOMAN
>   Look honey, it's that poor young
>   boy who tried to rob us.

>   OLD MAN
>   He still hasn't gotten himself
>   together.

>   OLD WOMAN
>   Nope.

                          OLD MAN
                Some animals can't be trained.

The couple sits at the far end of the car.

They all sit silently

David glances at them.

They are staring at him. The woman has her hand in her purse.

                          DAVID
                You know, I had an job interview
                today.

The couple is taken aback.

                          DAVID
                With the mayor's office. Yep, you
                could be looking at the next
                Communications Director at City
                Hall.

The couple looks at him like he's crazy.

                          DAVID
                It's true. I know you don't believe
                me, but it's true.
                     (beat)
                It's funny, I'm supposed to back up
                the mayor in everything he does --
                make layoffs sound like vacation --
                but I can't even use the subway
                system. Some New Yorker I am. How
                am I going to talk myself out of
                this one?

The train moves into the station. The old couple get up to
leave. No one is getting on.

                          OLD WOMAN
                Should we leave him alone? He could
                hurt himself.

                          OLD MAN
                He's a lost cause, Mable. Just let
                him be.

The old man steps off.

The doors close and the train leaves the station.

David rests again in his solitude.

LATER

David has fallen asleep. <u>It's been a long day.</u>

The subway train slowing to enter a new station wakes him.

The doors open and a FEW PEOPLE board the train along with a
TRANSIT OFFICER. <u>One who had chased David earlier.</u>

The transit officer looks at David suspiciously.

David looks at him through tired, blurry eyes.

<u>Realization</u> crosses both of their faces simultaneously.

The transit officer approaches David.

The doors to the subway train are still open.

The door warning CHIMES.

David bolts out the door.

The transit officer follows.

SUBWAY

> TRANSIT OFFICER
> (in walkie-talkie)
> This is officer 241, I'm chasing
> the Mole-Man. Request back-up!

David takes off running down a subway tunnel.

The transit officer in pursuit.

Two other officers join the chase.

> TRANSIT OFFICER
> Dispatch, the Mole-Man is moving
> south near 14th Street in the No. 6
> tunnel. He's got a gun.

The second officer, who has reached the first looks at him
questioningly.

The first transit officer, shrugs as if to say, "why not?"

Over their radios they hear:

> DISPATCH
> Suspect considered armed and
> dangerous. Permission to shoot to
> kill.

INT. DEPUTY MAYOR'S OFFICE - DAY

An official looking office.

Michael Overend is sitting behind his desk on the phone.

>   MICHAEL OVEREND
>   (on phone)
>   How long?
>   (beat)
>   Great. I'll be there.

He hangs up.

>   MICHAEL OVEREND
>   (shouting)
>   Doris! Call my next appointment...a
>   David Swanson. Please tell him, I
>   apologize but we will have to
>   reschedule.

>   DORIS (O.C.)
>   Yes sir.

Michael grabs his coat and exits the office.

INT. MAINTENANCE CLOSET

David has found a hiding place. An old maintenance closet.

>   DAVID
>   Jeez, could this day get any worse?

INT. CAB - DAY

Natalie is in the backseat of a cab. She has her tablet and
is writing.

The car radio is on.

>   RADIO ANNOUNCER
>   We interrupt for this special
>   report from WNYC.

>   ANCHOR
>   Good afternoon. The elusive and
>   dangerous subway Mole-Man is
>   seemingly only minutes from being
>   apprehended.

Natalie looks up and leans forward to listen.

                    ANCHOR
          Sources report that police are
          closing in on the vagrant, who is
          wanted for a series of vicious
          attacks and murders that have
          occurred over the past ten years.

                    NATALIE
          Would you mind turning that up
          please?

The CAB DRIVER turns up the volume.

                    ANCHOR
          As we speak, City Hall officials,
          along with the police commissioner,
          are gathering at the City Hall
          subway station. There, it is
          expected that police will deliver
          the dangerous Mole-Man in only
          minutes.

The cab driver peels out.

Natalie is tossed about in the backseat like a toy. She tries
to hold on.

                    NATALIE
          What are you doing?!

                    CAB DRIVER
          Must see the Mole-Man.

INT. MAINTENANCE CLOSET

The police are banging on the door.

                    TRANSIT OFFICER (O.C.)
          We know you're in there.

                    DAVID
          Think, David. Think.

INT. SUBWAY TUNNEL - SAME

The transit officers are pounding on the door with their
nightsticks.

                    TRANSIT OFFICER
          You've got one more chance or we're
          coming in.

More OFFICERS arrive with a battering ram. They prepare to
smash the door in.

TO DAVID

He is looking for a way out, but the room is sealed.

> DAVID
> Think, David.

He spots a small beat-up shovel.

INT. CAB - SAME

Traffic is gridlocked.

People are running by.

<u>In general, it's all-out commotion.</u>

> CAB DRIVER
> (out the window)
> Hang him!

> NATALIE
> Here.

She hands him $5.

> NATALIE
> I'll walk.

Natalie gets out of the cab.

INT. MAINTENANCE CLOSET

The door bust open and falls on the floor.

The transit officers come crashing into the room.

David is gone.

The transit officers are bewildered. <u>Where could he have escaped to?</u>

They exit the closet.

LATER

The door laying on the ground. MOVES.

Slowly, the door is being pushed up from below.

David dug a hole near the door and hid in it. The door covered the hole and David when it fell in.

David crawls out of the hole.

He peaks out of the closet to see the transit officers down the tunnel just a bit, searching with flashing lights.

David sneaks out.

He is spotted!

The chase begins again. David takes off running, officers in tow.

> TRANSIT OFFICER
> (into radio)
> Suspect is moving south again.

> DISPATCH
> (over radio)
> Block at Canal.

BLOCKADE

> POLICE 1
> Blockade in place.

David is running, periodically looking behind him.

Up ahead he spots more police.

He immediately makes a quick right and runs down a different tunnel.

EXT. CITY STREET - DAY

Natalie is running through a crowded street, pushing by people.

She runs over a subway grate.

David is directly beneath her, running through the tunnel.

EXT. CITY HALL - SAME

Natalie stops when she reaches City Hall.

There is a huge crowd of police, citizens, the MAYOR and Michael Overend.

> REPORTER
> Mr. Mayor, has the Mole-Man been captured?

                    MAYOR
          We can only say that we're
          confident that this criminal will
          not terrorize the people of this
          city for another night.

Natalie pushes her way up to the Mayor.

                    NATALIE
          Have you identified who he is?

                    MICHAEL OVEREND
          There will be a briefing soon. We
          cannot comment further at this
          time.

                    REPORTER 2
          Mr. Mayor, will the Mole-Man be
          taken alive?

                    MAYOR
          That's not my concern. Just as long
          as he's taken.

INT. SUBWAY TUNNEL

Everywhere David turns, more police are following.

He is funneled out a single exit.

Ahead, he sees a crowd cheering and jeering.

Behind, police are chasing.

When David reaches the street, the police tackle him right in
front of the Mayor.

David struggles, but he is overpowered and handcuffed.

Immediately, a pack of ravenous reporters, including Natalie
surround them. Cameras are CLICKING. Microphones are shoved
into his face.

Various TELEVISION REPORTERS are reporting LIVE from the
scene.

In the background, we see the struggle.

                    REPORTER 1
          As you see behind me, the Mole-Man
          is in custody.

                    REPORTER 2
          He's just as hideous as his
          description. The smell is
          horrendous.

                    REPORTER 3
          Sources tell us that the Mole-Man
          may have taken shots at the police
          during the chase. One officer has
          been wounded.

The police pull David to his feet.

David looks right at Natalie.

                    NATALIE
          David?

                    DAVID
          Thank God. Natalie.

                    MICHAEL OVEREND
          You know this man?

                    NATALIE
          David Swanson, what are you doing?

This rings a bell with the deputy mayor.

                    MICHAEL OVEREND
          David Swanson?

The man with the camera from the subway earlier jumps in
front of him and takes his picture.

                    DAVID
          Seriously?

                    MICHAEL OVEREND
          You're not the Mole-Man?

                    NATALIE
          Although you smell like him.

                    DAVID
          Nice to meet you, Mr. Deputy Mayor.
          David Swanson.

The old couple from earlier is in the crowd.

                    OLD WOMAN
          Can't wait to see how he gets out
          of this one.

                    OLD MAN
          Never happen.

                    OLD WOMAN
          Betcha 20.

                    OLD MAN
          You're on.

David turns to the Mayor.

                    DAVID
          Sir.

The Mayor turns to a policeman.

                    MAYOR
          What's going on here?

                    DAVID
          I'll tell you what's going on, sir.
          This morning, I was on my way to
          interview with your office.

                    MAYOR
          Interview?

                    DAVID
          Yes. Communications director.

                    NATALIE
          And this is how you dress?

                    DAVID
          Since I had a few hours before the
          interview, I decided to conduct
          some research. I went underground
          to look at the city from a
          different perspective. You should
          try it sometime, Mr. Mayor. Just
          when you think you really know
          something, turn it over. Look at it
          from the other side.

David turns to the reporters. They press in on him and push
microphones in his face.

                    DAVID
          You know, a city is like a...ah
          ...a person really. It has a heart,
          a soul, a personality. But it also
          has bowels. Now, many people don't
          like to talk about bowels or even
          acknowledge that they exist.
                    (MORE)

                    DAVID (CONT'D)
      But they're a necessity.
          (beat)
      New York has bowels. I spent my day
      in these bowels and I'm here to say
      that I'm, well, impressed.

                    REPORTER 1
      With what in particular?

                    REPORTER 2
      What did you find?

INT. UNDERGROUND ROOM

Papa, Bullet, Mandy, Jessica and the others are sitting
around a small television watching the live news report.

David is being interviewed --

                    DAVID
      A small community of vital,
      hardworking New Yorkers trying to
      make ends meet. Trying to take
      pride in their community, trying to
      put food on the...ah...crate or
      whatever. And you know the worst
      part? The worst part is that these
      are the forgotten New Yorkers.
      Their contributions are ignored day
      after day, much as their pleas for
      a spare dime are ignored in front
      of The Dakota on a rainy Monday
      morning.
          (beat)
      These people are as much a part of
      the New York community as you and
      me. Yet, they endure constant
      harassment, constant persecution,
      and -- even worse -- constant
      dehumanization. I, no we, at City
      Hall...

EXT. CITY HALL - SAME

He glances at the Mayor and Michael, who are uneasy with what
he might say.

                    DAVID
      ...believe it's time to acknowledge
      the contributions of our houseless
      neighbors.

                    MAYOR
               (to Overend)
          Who is this guy?

The old man hands his wife a $20 bill.

                    DAVID
          Granted, it's not perfect down
          there, just as it's not perfect up
          here. Some of these people need our
          help. Others are as self-sufficient
          as Donald Trump.

                    REPORTER 2
          Donald Trump lives down there?

                    REPORTER 3
          No, he just owns the bedrock.

                    DAVID
          It won't be an easy task. And we
          need to get started now. Indeed,
          drug use is widespread. Many could
          benefit from some sort of
          counseling. It will have to be done
          on a case-by-case basis. That's why
          we at the mayor's office are about
          to outline a five-step plan to
          ensure that all New Yorkers who
          want housing will have the
          opportunity to obtain it.

                    REPORTER 1
          Mr. Mayor, is this true?

                    MAYOR
               (caught off-guard)
          Details will be
          released...ah...soon.

                    DAVID
          The key is that we learn to
          understand one another. Indeed, I
          did this today because we believe
          we must reach into this community
          and embrace it. Only then will New
          Yorkers of all types and income
          levels live in harmony.

                    MAYOR
               (to Overend)
          He's good.

                    DAVID
          What I found today is what makes
          New York the greatest city in the
          universe. The diversity, the
          uniqueness...the on-time subway
          service.

                    MICHAEL OVEREND
          Thank you David.

Micahel, who had been growing increasingly uneasy about the
situation, tries to pull David aside.

David is exhausted and starting to babble.

                    DAVID
          The friendly people, the clean
          public restrooms. New York is just
          as intriguing and just as
          electrifying below the ground as it
          is above ground. Without the idiot
          landlords.

Michael jumps in and pulls David aside. David keeps talking.

                    DAVID
          And with a commitment from the
          mayor to improve services to the
          homeless, it will only get better.

The reporters turn their attention to the Mayor.

                    REPORTER 1
          Mr. Mayor, can you make this
          commitment?

                    MICHAEL OVEREND
               (to reporters)
          The mayor will have more to say
          about this later.

Michael pulls David aside.

                    MICHAEL OVEREND
               (to police officer)
          Can we get this cuffs off him?

The Mayor exits with the reporters following.

Michael and Natalie stay behind with David.

                    MICHAEL OVEREND
          Five-step program? What did you
          have in mind?

                    DAVID
          Step one: Acknowledge the problem.
          Step two: Make up four more steps.

                    MICHAEL OVEREND
          I think this is the beginning of a
          beautiful career in public service.
          Let's talk tomorrow at noon?

                    DAVID
          Done.

                    MICHAEL OVEREND
          Do me a favor, though.

                    DAVID
          What's that.

                    MICHAEL OVEREND
          Take a cab?

                    DAVID
          No doubt.

Michael leaves David and Natalie to return the Mayor's side
who is still being harassed by the reporters.

                    NATALIE
          All of that was bull wasn't it?

                    DAVID
          Think I aced the interview.

                    NATALIE
          Amazing. Well your crap may not
          stink but you sure do.

                    DAVID
          What? I shouldn't meet your parents
          like this?

                    NATALIE
          Let's get you cleaned up.

The two walk along the street.

                    NATALIE
          By the way, if you're not the Mole-
          Man, then who is?

                    DAVID
          After spending all day in these
          tunnels, I can guarantee that the
          Mole-Man is simply a figment of the
          city's imagination.

                    NATALIE
          Is that so?

David nods.

                    NATALIE
          In that case, sleep well New York.

As David and Natalie pass, a manhole cover behind them pops
up.

A man matching the Mole-Man's description -- and is the
homeless man who gave David his phone back -- pokes his head
out.

The Mole-Man smiles then goes back underground.

                    DAVID
          Sleep well indeed.

                              FADE TO BLACK.

www.ingramcontent.com/pod-product-compliance
Lightning Source LLC
Chambersburg PA
CBHW050012110426
42741CB00037B/3283